P9-AGM-105

# Crack of the Bat: The Louisville Slugger® Story

*Play Ball!,*

*Bob Hill*

BY BOB HILL

A **SPORTS**MASTERS Book

Sports Publishing Inc.
www.sportspublishinginc.com

# A **SPORTS**MASTERS Book

Sports Publishing Inc.
804 North Neil
Champaign, Illinois 61820

©2000 Hillerich & Bradsby Co.
All Rights Reserved.

Director of Production: Susan M. McKinney
Book design, project manager: Jennifer Layne Polson
Cover design: Terry Neutz Hayden
Copy editor: David Hamburg

ISBN: 1-58382-012-4

Printed in the USA.

*For my father, Bob Hill Sr., who spoke often of baseball, Bill Dickey and Ted Williams.*

## ACKNOWLEDGMENTS

**m**y biggest worry about this book is not what it contains, but who or what might have been left out. The history of the Hillerich & Bradsby Company—and its Louisville Slugger—is so rich and deep, it wasn't possible to name all of the employees who helped make this book possible.

On the writing end, I especially want to thank my *Courier-Journal* colleagues C. Ray Hall, who helped edit the original manuscript, and Pam Spaulding, who helped with many of the photographs. Special thanks also to Cara Bernosky of IMC Licensing, who kept the project rounding the bases when home plate seemed so far away.

I also want to thank the staff of the *Courier-Journal* library, Andy Anderson and his staff at the University of Louisville Photo Archives and Tom Owen and his staff at the University of Louisville Record Archives, along with Jennifer Layne Polson of Sports Publishing Inc., the book's designer and project manager, Tom Bast, acqisitions and developmental editor and Terry Neutz Hayden, dustjacket designer and Louisville native.

Thanks also to Phyllis Roberts, Walter Barney, JoAnne Bickel Feldman, Sherri Pawson, Stephen Reily, David Quentin Voight, *Louisville* magazine, the Baseball Hall of Fame, Cooperstown, the Society of American Baseball Research, Bill Williams, Mike McGrath, Chuck Schupp, Rex Bradley, Jack Norton and the many employees at Hillerich & Bradsby who went way beyond the call of duty to make this book a tribute to their Louisville Slugger.

# CONTENTS

I never expected to be a major league baseball player. It didn't seem possible. Our family—my parents, one sister and three brothers—had lived on a small farm near Ekron, Kentucky. In 1925, when I was seven years old, we moved to Louisville.

That was a different time. Kids were expected to help the family and we all pitched in. I had a paper route, delivered box lunches and also played softball and baseball whenever I could.

I loved sports, but was only 5 feet 5 inches tall and weighed about 110 pounds when I graduated from Manual High School. I'd been hurt my senior year, and played in only five baseball games. Playing professional baseball never entered my mind.

I got a job at a box factory making 25 cents an hour, then went to work as an apprentice cable splicer for the telephone company. I was making $18 a week and playing baseball in my church league in Shawnee Park and other places on weekends.

In 1938, a guy named Cap Neal, the general manager of the AAA Louisville Colonels, saw something he liked and signed me for $150 a month. Three years later, I was in Yankee Stadium playing shortstop for the Brooklyn Dodgers in the 1941 World Series. I remember looking around and thinking, "What am I doing here?"

I enjoyed my career with the Dodgers. I was very fortunate to be playing alongside men like Duke Snider, Roy Campanella, Don Newcombe, Carl Erskine, Gil Hodges, Billy Cox and Jackie Robinson, and we ended up playing in the World Series seven times.

While playing with the Colonels, I first met the Hillerichs—Bud Hillerich, Ward Hillerich and Junie Hillerich. I signed my first bat contract with Hillerich & Bradsby in September 1938. At first I used a Vince Sherlock-model bat. Then the company helped me design my own bat, an R-46, which I used the first year I hit .300. My first bats said "Hal Reese" on them because that's how I was known back then.

My relationship with Hillerich & Bradsby has always been great. They treated me with great bats and, as I needed them, with great golf clubs. After retiring from baseball, and then broadcasting major league games with Curt Gowdy and Dizzy Dean, I was asked by Jack Hillerich to represent the company at the World Series, All-Star Games, spring training and other baseball events.

Hillerich & Bradsby is dedicated to the players, and to manufacturing the finest bats that can be made. I'm proud to have been a part of this company for these many years.

Sincerely,

*"Pee Wee" Reese*

Pee Wee Reese

**B**aseball—more than any other sport—allows us to play catch with the past. We can stand in the present, the wonderful era of Sammy Sosa, Mark McGwire, Derek Jeter and Ken Griffey Jr., and feel their connection to Henry Aaron, Mickey Mantle, Babe Ruth and Frank "Home Run" Baker. We can sit in a darkened theater and cry as Kevin Costner plays catch with his father's ghost in "Field of Dreams." We can pass on this same spirit to our children: true happiness is your daughter rounding third and the left fielder still chasing the ball.

For more than 100 years, baseball's connecting thread has been the Louisville Slugger. Its proud sponsor has been the Hillerich & Bradsby Company, and the Hillerich family, who has kept the dream alive for five generations—and counting. How many other American companies or families can claim that kinship with history?

Writing this book has been an absolute joy. It's allowed me to revisit baseball's roots and talk to its greatest players. It's allowed me to meet men and women who still take enormous pride in their product. It's allowed me to play catch with the memory of my father, who first taught me how to throw a baseball, took me to Yankee Stadium, and bought me peanuts and Cracker Jacks, and my first Louisville Slugger.

May the circle be unbroken.

*Bob Hill*

Bob Hill

CRACK OF THE BAT:
THE LOUISVILLE SLUGGER
STORY

 O N E

# OUT AT THE
# OLD BAT GAME

A Pitch and a Swing.
With a mighty swing frozen in time, Babe Ruth changed baseball and sports history forever.

**b**aseball bats—in various forms and fashions—have been evolving in this country since about the time the first settlers from England moved into what would become Boston, then decided what the city really needed was a ballpark with a short left-field fence.

Historians agree that baseball had its general origin in a pair of games brought here by those British. The first was cricket, an adult, cultured game with its innings, manicured grounds, umpires, distinctive bat and "spot of tea." The second game was rounders, a rougher, backyard game played by eager children striking a crude ball with a rounded stick—often swung with one hand.

The more aristocratic cricket used a flat-sided bat, which sometimes made its way into the backyard games. But rounders was played mostly with a club of a different sort, an old tree limb made round on a foot-powered lathe, or perhaps an old wagon tongue trimmed smooth, with a knob on the end to keep it from slipping away.

The original balls were made of anything—from tightly wound twine to balled-up sheepskin to rags wrapped around a walnut. Once this lopsided ball was struck with a bat, it would serve no purpose to just stand and watch it fly; the urge was to run to a base while someone else chased down the ball. Three left turns around the bases and you were "home" again. Could Lou Brock be far behind?

In their book *Baseball—An Illustrated History*, historians Ken Burns and Geoffrey C. Ward tell us these early games of "paddle-ball," "old cat," "three old cat," "base" and "Base Ball" evolved in a dozen different directions, with not all the players following the same base paths.

Revolutionary War soldiers played a version of the game at Valley Forge. Legendary explorers Meriwether Lewis and William Clark tried to teach the "game of base" to the Nez Perce Indians while coming home from what might have been baseball's first really long road trip.

In the early 1800s, New England "town ball" became the game's most popular form. It was generally played on a square field with no foul lines and anywhere from eight to 15 men on a side—with room for 50 if the occasion demanded it, the earliest version of the "Ted Williams shift." The winner was the first team to score a set number of runs, often 21.

The pitcher was called the "feeder." It was his job to feed the ball to the "striker"—who could call for a pitch anyplace he wanted it, and could wait all day until he got it. Old drawings of the era show the bats to be heavy, thick and barely tapered, probably made of hickory, willow or ash. One of the more charming aspects of town ball was that fielders could throw the ball at a runner, who was declared out if so "soaked."

Those were simpler times; the batter was out if a ball was caught in the air or on the first bounce. No one in that early era wore gloves; the ball was soft and wasn't hit that hard. Besides, gloves weren't considered manly.

One of baseball's enduring myths is that Abner Doubleday, who would later go on to West Point and glory as a Civil War soldier, drew up the first comprehensive rules for this unruly pastime in 1839. It is a fine story, but a historical whiff; Doubleday never claimed the honor and quite possibly never even held a bat.

Experts now agree that baseball took its biggest strides in the 1840s, when a New York City shipping clerk named Alexander Cartwright helped

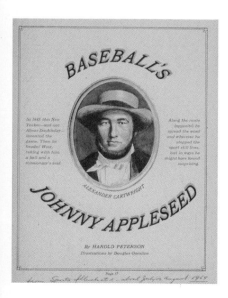

**The Beginning.**
*New York shipping clerk Alexander Cartwright got baseball on the right path.*

*Crack of the Bat: The Louisville Slugger Story*

form the New York Knickerbocker Base Ball Club. The original rules included eight men to a side, a diamond-shaped infield and the establishment of a "foul" territory. This was to be a "gentleman's game"; no one should ever be paid to play baseball. Indeed, throwing the ball at the runner was outlawed, considerably reducing contusions.

The more formal New York game spread like summer wildfire across the country and into Canada. The Civil War took baseball—along with muskets—into the Deep South, where soldiers would write home of fine games interrupted by untimely gunfire, and Abraham Lincoln and his son took in games behind the White House.

When the war ended, the returning veterans spread baseball across the land. In the next 20 years, almost every town had a team, colleges began to challenge one another, barnstorming women's teams were formed and the best of the players were paid for their work. Professional baseball was here to stay.

Baseball rules—and equipment—continued to evolve with the help of Dr. Daniel Adams, a Harvard graduate. Adams was a contemporary of Cartwright, who in 1849 had left the Knickerbockers for the California Gold Rush, a route followed by the Brooklyn Dodgers and New York Giants a century or so later.

Adams added a ninth baseball position—the shortstop. The catcher stood 20 feet behind the batter, catching balls on the first bounce. The

**Civil War.** *Baseball marched southward during the Civil War as Union prisoners demonstrated the game to their captors.*

first, second and third basemen set up defensive shop by standing right on their respective bases—which were 12 inches square. Home "plate" was often just that—a circular piece of iron about 15 inches in diameter.

By 1863, a single umpire was allowed to call strikes and, perhaps more important, the "balls"—although in the early days of baseball it might require nine balls to earn a walk. By the mid-1860s, fly balls had to be caught in the air; the first bounce was no longer sufficient. By the 1880s, pitchers were throwing overhand. Still—at least until the late 1880s—the batters were allowed to designate their own strike zones—either high or low. It was 1893 when the current distance from the pitcher to the batter—60 feet 6 inches—was established.

According to *Baseball—An Illustrated History*, Doc Adams also gave the game another legacy—a better ball to hit. The Knickerbockers had used a ball so light, it couldn't be thrown 200 feet—the original Wiffle ball. The doctor said he made his own balls for years with several ounces of rubber cuttings wound with yarn and covered with leather. Then he found a saddle-maker who was able to stitch up the balls more tightly with horsehide, giving them more distance and durability.

by the 1850s, commercially produced baseballs with rubber cores were being made in New York, and by the 1880s, baseballs with rubber cores wrapped in yarn and covered with animal hide were machine-made by the thousands. The ball was about the same size and weight as it is today, but not as consistently hard. It was not until 1911, when the cork-centered ball came into the game, that the home run was much of a factor. The effect was immediate: Frank "Home Run" Baker went from hitting two home runs in 1910 to 11 in 1911.

That may not sound like much, but using the same arithmetic, imagine Mark McGwire or Sammy Sosa hitting 385 home runs in one year—up from a mere 70.

Before the advent of the cork-center ball, fields were often designed without fences; advancing the runner was important. The hitting philosophy of the day was espoused by Wee Willie Keeler, who batted .343 in a major league career lasting from 1892 to 1910: "Hit 'em where they ain't."

Meanwhile, the changes in bats had come more slowly. Grainy photographs of those Victorian days showed young men in beards and young women in long, billowing dresses wielding bats that looked like elongated, slightly tapered rolling pins.

It was already obvious that baseball had a powerful effect on children and young adults. It required little equipment, kept them moving outdoors and required enough skill to keep it interesting—and competitive. The early game could be played in yards, alleys, streets, school yards and parks. Most who played the game had enough skill to relate to those who were better, to appreciate what it took to strike a moving ball with a moving bat.

There were no size restrictions on bats until 1859, when a professional committee ruled they could be no larger than 2.5 inches in diameter. That was changed in 1895, when the "modern" bat was standardized: "The bat must be round, not over 2 3/4 inches in diameter nor more than 42 inches in length, and entirely of hardwood, except that for a distance of 18 inches from

**A Legendary Baseball.**
*Hitting a cork-center ball like the one pictured above, Babe Ruth walloped more home runs in a month than earlier sluggers could hit in a whole year.*

*Crack of the Bat: The Louisville Slugger Story*

the end, twine may be wound or a granulated substance applied to the handle."

The new rule did not mention a maximum weight, pine tar or George Brett. Those early sluggers would lug semi-tree trunks weighing as much as 48 ounces to the plate, far heavier than the 32- to 34-ounce bats favored today.

New York bat manufacturers were so desperate for raw material in those days that A.G. Spalding ran newspaper ads seeking wood. One book on baseball history—*Banana Bats and Ding-Dong Balls* by Dan Gutman—shows an ad seeking 100,000 wagon tongues "made from well-seasoned, second-growth ash, free from knots and blemishes"—the first-ever Conestoga-model bat.

According to Gutman, the first known patent for a multi-sport bat was issued in 1864 to a Philip Caminoni. The bat would be made of a wood frame covered with donkey, pig or other animal skin, and it was less than likely to stand up to a Walter Johnson fastball, much less Roger Clemens's.

**Boys at Play.**
*Baseball became popular because all a kid needed was a bat, a ball, a glove and an open field.*

Patent 1926
Patent 1936
Patent 1937

*Although simple in theory, many variations of baseball bats have been patented over the years.*

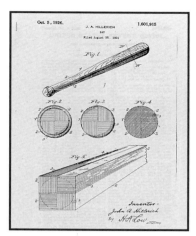
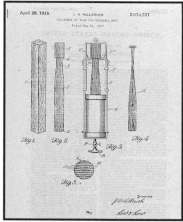
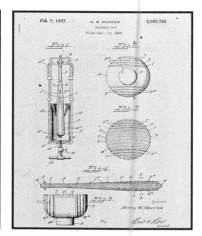

**Early Glove.**
*Early players such as Al Buelmiller used gloves not much larger than a bare hand.*

Speaking of which, the first paper bat was patented in 1884. Its inventor, William Williams, hoped his bat would not split or break, the "crack" of the bat apparently to be replaced with more of a "thwop." He did have an accidental eye on history, however; he thought his bat could be strengthened by molding the paper around metal, never imagining the day when aluminum would dominate the industry.

In the late 1800s and early 1900s, the famed "banana bat" made its patented appearance. Its inventor, Emile Kinst, said he hoped his curved bat would cause the ball to spin, making it more difficult to catch. Fine for golf, but his bat never caught on.

J.A. "Bud" Hillerich also got into the bat patenting business, as did his Hillerich & Bradsby Company over the years. At first thought, patenting a bat seems a little like trying to patent a golf tee; how much new can you do with it? But Hillerich's patents—including his cork handle—were successful, as were those of company engineers trying to design a better way to process, protect and reshape bats. These ideas also made for very interesting patent drawings—practically works of art themselves—with the various designs giving baseball a scientific look far removed from the sheer instincts involved in playing the game well.

Baseball gloves also evolved over the years, beginning with an era in the 1870s when ballplayers would actually catch fly balls in their hats, no doubt stretching a cap size to about 12 $\frac{7}{8}$ by season's end.

The very early gloves—and players using them were often considered wimps and sissies—left the fingers exposed, protecting only the palms. Full-fingered gloves developed from the earlier style, but early gloves still weren't much bigger than a player's hand, and offered little protection. The whole concept that a glove should be built to bushel-basket-sized dimensions to aid in fielding a ball didn't fully develop until the 1950s.

According to *Banana Bats and Ding-Dong Balls*, the last ballplayer to play the game barehanded was Jeremiah Denny, who played for Louisville in the 1880s and 1890s. Denny was the rarest of players, an ambidextrous third baseman who, because he could throw with either hand, never had to backhand a ball.

*Crack of the Bat: The Louisville Slugger Story*

Rogers Hornsby.
*He began the trend away from "bottle bats" to more tapered models with smaller handles .*

**Bullpen.**
*The American Tobacco Company—the manufacturer of Bull Durham tobacco—put up a big bull sign in almost every minor and major baseball park in the country in the area where the pitchers warmed up—hence the name "bullpen." A ball batted against the sign netted a player $25. This photo was taken in Louisville's Eclipse Park in 1914.*

In the early 1900s—influenced by legendary players Rogers Hornsby and Babe Ruth—bats finally took on a more streamlined look. Those changes were well documented by Jack McGrath, an advertising and media relations employee of Hillerich & Bradsby Company, a direct descendant of the company J. F. Hillerich had founded in Louisville.

McGrath said changes in bats came slowly until Hornsby began his career in 1915. Before Hornsby, most bats had large handles and relatively small barrels. They tapered a little from barrel to handle, with the weight much more evenly distributed than it was with modern bats.

That was classic "hit and run" baseball; get on base using short, accurate swings with wide, heavy bats. Hitters such as Ty Cobb, who has the highest career average in baseball history (.367) and the second-highest hit total (4,191), held his hands three or four inches apart and slapped at pitches. His bat was 34 $\frac{1}{2}$ inches long and weighed 40 ounces.

By contrast, Rod Carew (.328 lifetime) swung a 34 $\frac{1}{2}$-inch bat weighing 32 ounces, and Ted Williams (.344 lifetime) wielded a 35-inch bat weighing 33 ounces. In the modern era, most bats weigh about 32 ounces and are 33 to 34 inches long—the general rule of thumb being that a bat weighing two ounces less than its length is about right.

"We look back on the Hornsby model as marking a definite transition from the old to the new," McGrath wrote in a letter to a New York sportswriter. "The Hornsby model—as compared to the earlier models—had a comparatively large barrel tapering gracefully to a comparatively small handle.

"When Babe Ruth came along, however, his model was far more streamlined than the Hornsby, with a barrel at its largest part about as large as Hornsby's and with a taper to a very small handle."

**The Long and Short of It.**
*At the 1946 Annual Baseball Convention in Los Angeles, Jack McGarth (left) of Hillerich & Bradsby Company shows the longest and shortest bat models ever made to Cliff Kachline (right) of The Sporting News.*

Until Ruth began hitting more home runs in one month than other sluggers were hitting in an entire season, bats weighing 40 ounces or more were commonplace. Ruth, Cobb, Eddie Collins, George Sisler, Nap Lajoie and Tris Speaker all used them.

Ruth used bats weighing from 40 to 43 ounces in 1919, when he hit 29 home runs. His bats weighed from 40 to 47 ounces, when he hit 54 homers in 1920, and his bats weighed 39 to 42 ounces in 1927, when he hit 60 home runs.

"Ruth," wrote McGrath, "swung from the heels whereas the high batting average man before him, and also his early contemporaries, concentrated on getting on first.

"Younger players and future major leaguers started to copy the Ruth swing, but lacking the tremendous swinging power of the Babe, they found that they could accomplish this only by using a much lighter bat."

The Babe changed the bat-making business. Other players stopped choking up on the bat and began holding it at the very end. They began using longer and longer bats, hoping to cover as much ground as possible: "Swing and pray for a ball out of the park," wrote McGrath.

Ruth's influence was so great that established hitters such as Hornsby—who holds the major league record for the highest single-season batting average (.424)—went from hitting nine home runs in 1920 to slugging 21 in 1921 and 42 in 1922. He even hit 25 home runs in 1924, the year he batted .424.

**A Line of Louisville Sluggers.**
*Seeking safety in numbers, these Hillerich & Bradsby executives hung out their bats for all to see.*

Jay Kirke and Jack Bentley.
*Two old-timers—Jay Kirke and
Jack Bentley—strike classic bat
poses in this 1920s photo
snapped in Louisville.*

Gus Felix, c. 1920s.
*Brooklyn Dodger Gus Felix
had a wide variety of bats
to choose from.*

According to McGrath, the shortest major league bat Hillerich & Bradsby ever made was a 30-inch Louisville Slugger turned for Harry Hinchman, who—appropriately enough—would have 11 hits and bat .216 in a 15-game major league career with Cleveland in 1907.

The longest-bat award went to Al "Bucketfoot Al" Simmons, who batted .334 over a 20-year Hall of Fame career while swinging a 38 $^3/_4$-inch bat that might have created a strong-enough draft to give the first baseman a head cold.

By the 1920s the players had a wide variety of bats from which to choose, as shown in the accompanying photograph of Gus Felix, who played outfield for the Braves and Dodgers from 1923 to 1927. The variety didn't help him much; he hit .274 in a 583-game major league career, including 12 home runs, 48 less than Ruth hit in one season.

The heaviest bat went to—who else?—The Babe, who once ordered a 54-ounce bat, although no one knows if he ever dragged it up to the plate, leaving a weaving trail in the dust behind him. The most consistent "Hercules of Heft" was Ed Roush, who got into the Hall of Fame using bats in the 44- to 50-ounce range. Incredibly, his bats were only 33 inches long, giving them the appearance of well-sanded logs.

Roush—not the most patient of hitters—used his cudgels to slap hits to all fields and was credited one year with getting seven hits on pitchouts, including a triple. McGrath said the lightest Louisville Slugger professional bats ever made went to Alvin Dark: 28 ounces.

The thinnest and thickest handles belong to the models of two all-time greats. Stan Musial's personal model was only $^{15}/_{16}$ths of an inch at its thinnest point—and he would shave it down from there. "Shoeless" Joe Jackson's bat was 1 $^3/_8$ inches at its handle.

In the 1950s, McGrath noticed a slight trend toward longer bats. He worried that added wind resistance might actually slow a bat, cutting down any advantage it already had. It was a point now taken as gospel: Bat speed has the most effect on distance; a heavier bat swung at a slower speed can have less pop than a lighter bat swung at a faster speed.

His analysis foreshadowed a problem that bat manufacturers have to deal with today: Slimmer bats with thinner handles in the hands of bigger, stronger players are more liable to break; there's no way to avoid it.

The 1960s also brought artificial-turf infields, which placed more emphasis on speed and hitting the ball through the infield. Lighter bats, more easily handled, were more in vogue. There was a brief revival of heavier bats in the 1960s, with Rusty Staub using a 36-inch bat, and Dick Allen swinging a 40-ounce blunderbuss. Roberto Clemente had a 39-ounce bat and even Tony Oliva had a 36-ounce bat. But bats would get thinner and lighter afterward.

The most dramatic changes in bats came in the 1960s and early '70s, as aluminum bats pounded their way into baseball and softball, changing those games forever.

According to *Banana Bats and Ding-Dong Balls*, the aluminum-making process was actually patented in 1886, only two years after Bud Hillerich made the first Louisville Slugger.

But aluminum didn't take flight until World War II, with the creation of faster, lighter airplanes. Baseball bats entered the picture in the late 1960s, when Anthony Merola, a Pennsylvania pool cue manufacturer, thought the same process might work for bats.

b y 1969, aluminum bats were being used in softball. Little League baseball approved them in 1971, and the NCAA began using them in 1975. In an incredibly short period of time, aluminum bats took over the amateur game, which it still dominates.

In fact, the Sporting Goods Manufacturers Association reported that, as of 1998, aluminum bats accounted for about 90 percent of the more than $115 million bat market.

But the transition wasn't easy. In their early years, aluminum bats were mostly thought of as a much more durable, cheaper substitute for white ash. But with a little tinkering it also became obvious they could propel a baseball where no cowhide had gone before.

The first aluminum bats were heavy and awkward to use. As bats were made increasingly lighter, they delivered more pop. A 34-inch aluminum bat could weigh as little as 26 ounces, dimensions almost impossible to get with wood. As lightweight aerospace alloys such as C405 and scandium—available only from the baseball mecca of Ukraine—were developed, the bat's "trampoline" effect was magnified. In addition, these alloys were woven to form thinner bat barrels, and some barrels were filled with compressed gas inside to heighten the trampoline effect.

Both wooden and aluminum bats actually bend back upon contact, like slightly bowed sticks. With wooden bats, it was the ball that absorbed most of the impact. With aluminum bats, the metal absorbed more impact, meaning the baseball lost less kinetic energy, and roared away about 10 percent faster—and farther—than if struck by wood.

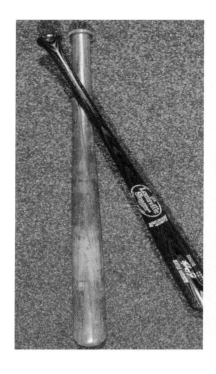

**Bats Old and New.**
*This sleek black model and an old-time bat stained by time—if not by tobacco juice—shows the bat's evolution.*

**The Aluminum Bat.**
*Manufacturing the inevitable product of a modern high-tech society, Hillerich & Bradsby now sells millions of aluminum bats.*

Aluminum bats were also more forgiving; a ball hit near the handle would have a better chance of finding a hole in the infield, even flying over the fence. Its "balance point" could be moved around to add momentum, and its "sweet spot" seemed to be larger. Aluminum bats cost a lot more—anywhere from $100 to $250—but their effectiveness and durability made them worth the cost. Baseball bats, largely unchanged since J. F. Hillerich's shop had turned its first about 100 years earlier, had rocketed into space-age technology.

Major league baseball—and its minor leagues—remained firmly in the grip of wooden bats. Placing aluminum bats in the hands of players as strong as Sammy Sosa, Mark McGwire and Junior Griffey was beyond comprehension; hitting records would be destroyed daily.

But not all college, high school and amateur coaches were pleased with the metal product. Some coaches worried about player safety; baseballs seemed to be flying back at the pitcher and infielders more quickly. Many coaches also worried about "the integrity of the game." Their contests were increasingly being dominated by the long ball, becoming too long, as more and more runs were scored. Many baseball fans, however, enjoyed the show, as did the players.

In 1988, as it became obvious that aluminum had added a boost to the game, an NCAA committee slowed the push for ever lighter, quicker bats by mandating a maximum length-to-weight differential of five—meaning a 34-inch aluminum bat could not weigh less than 29 ounces.

Still, the home runs came. In 1997, NCAA Division I teams hit an average of 1.06 home runs a game, up from .70 in 1995. The College World Series set records for home runs in 1995 and 1998, and in 1998, the University of Southern California beat Arizona State 21-14, in the title game of a championship series that saw 62 home runs hit and 41 offensive records broken.

It was that "five touchdown" game that caught the eye of aluminum bat critics. The Cape Cod League and several NCAA Division II leagues returned to wooden bats and saw batting averages and home runs plummet. Meanwhile, the NCAA and the National Federation of State High School Associations, Little League Baseball and other amateur leagues commissioned a study by the National Institute for Sports Study and Safety at Brown University to measure bat performance.

Its tests confirmed much higher "exit" speeds with aluminum bats. For example, the average speed of a ball hit with a wooden bat was 87.5 miles an hour, while four aluminum bats tested at 95 mph and one aluminum bat registered a speed of 105 mph. All told, 76 percent of the "best" hits in its test came off metal, 24 percent from wood.

Jim Sherwood, a mechanical engineering professor at the University of Massachusetts at Lowell, began doing similar tests. His tests were done on a Baum Hitting Machine with one wooden bat and one metal bat. The baseballs were clocked at 70 miles an hour, with bat tip speed reaching 85 miles an hour. The ball velocity was 75 to 94 mph off the wooden bat, and from 100 to 105 mph with the metal bat.

"The testing of aluminum bats started out as a safety issue with the NCAA," Sherwood said, "but their own statistics have shown baseball is one of the safest college sports."

Thus the new aluminum bat standards, according to Ty Halpin, who works for the NCAA as a liaison between the organization and the schools, are aimed primarily at protecting the integrity of the game, keeping more baseballs in the park.

"Technology kept improving," he said. "They kept hitting the ball further. We wanted to stop the arms race between the bat companies."

In a sense, amateur baseball was trying to again bring the game full circle, to develop aluminum bats that behaved more like wooden bats. In 1999 the NCAA reduced the bat diameter from 2 3/4 inches to 2 5/8 inches and mandated that the difference between a bat's length and weight could not be more than three units (i.e., a 34-inch bat couldn't weigh less than 31 ounces). The National Federation of State High School Associations changed its bats so they would fit the same specifications—effective in the 2001 season.

Another goal for high schools and colleges—very difficult to reach, given the varying abilities and strengths of the players—was to make sure that the exit speed of a ball struck by a metal bat was about 94 miles an hour.

The change in NCAA regulations led to lawsuits filed by certain bat companies that argued that they would be stuck with older-model metal bats that couldn't be sold; but Halpin said the easing in of the new regulations has minimized that problem.

"We believed there was still enough market for the older bats that they could be sold," he said.

Meanwhile, baseball science marches on. Hillerich & Bradsby—among other bat manufacturers—is steadily working on "composite" bats made of wood and high-tech fibers that will be as durable as metal, yet give back to the game the "crack of the bat" at all levels.

"At some point," Sherwood said, "I think you'll see both composite and aluminum bats being used a lot."

The evolution of the bat has paralleled—if not influenced—the changes in the game. Here, from the 10th edition of *The Baseball Encyclopedia*—are rules changes that have had the greatest impact on hitters, umpires and the strike zone.

## EVOLUTION OF BASEBALL RULES

|  |  |
|---|---|
| 1880 | Base on balls on eight balls instead of nine. |
| | Catcher must catch ball on a fly to retire batter on a strikeout. |
| 1881 | Pitcher's box located 50 feet from home plate instead of 45 feet. |
| 1882 | Base on balls on seven balls. |
| 1883 | Foul ball caught on the first bounce is no longer an out. |
| 1884 | Pitcher's motion limited to shoulder-high delivery, instead of a delivery where the hand must pass below the hip. |
| | Base on balls on six balls. |
| 1885 | A portion of one side of the bat may be flat instead of round. |
| 1886 | Pitcher's box changed to 4 X 7 feet instead of 6 X 6 feet. |
| | Base on balls on seven balls. |
| 1887 | Batter no longer allowed to call for a high or low pitch. |
| | Strike zone defined as the area between the top of the shoulder and the bottom of the knee. |
| | Pitcher's box changed to 4 X 5 $\frac{1}{2}$ feet. |
| | Batter hit by pitched ball entitled to first base and not charged with a time at bat. |
| | Base on balls on five balls. |
| | Batter's base on balls credited as a hit and charged as a time at bat. |
| | Strikeout on four strikes instead of three strikes, where the first called third strike does not count. |
| 1888 | Batter's base on balls not a hit or time at bat. |
| | Batter credited with a hit if runner struck by batted ball. |
| | Strikeout on three strikes. |
| | Ground-rule double instead of home run if the ball is batted over the fence in fair territory where the fence is less than 210 feet from home plate. |
| 1889 | Base on balls with four balls. |
| 1891 | Any player may be substituted during a game, but the player substituted for may not reenter the game. (Before this, substitutions could be made only in the case of an injury or with permission of the opposing team.) |

*Crack of the Bat: The Louisville Slugger Story*

| 1892 | Ground-rule double if the ball is hit over the fence in fair territory where the fence is less than 235 feet from home plate. |
| 1893 | Pitching distance lengthened to 60 feet 6 inches, and marked by a rubber slab 12 inches long and 4 inches wide. |
| | The bat must be completely round. |
| 1894 | Batter charged with strike for hitting a foul bunt. |
| 1895 | Pitcher's rubber enlarged to 24 X 6 inches. |
| | Maximum diameter of bat increased from $2\frac{1}{2}$ inches to $2\frac{3}{4}$ inches. |
| | Batter automatically out on an infield fly when there is one out and first base is occupied. |
| | Strike charged to a batter on foul tip. |
| 1900 | Home plate changed from a 12-inch square to a 5-sided figure 17 inches wide. |
| 1901 | Infield fly rule changed to be in effect when there are no outs, as well as when there is one out. |
| | Any foul ball not caught on a fly is a strike unless the batter has two strikes on him (National League). |
| 1903 | Pitcher's mound must not be higher than 15 inches above the base lines and home plate. |
| | Any foul ball not caught on a fly is a strike unless the batter has two strikes on him (American League). |
| 1920 | The spitball and other unorthodox deliveries abolished. Special provision made to allow each team to name two pitchers as spitball pitchers for the 1920 season and thereafter no spitballers will be allowed. |
| | A ball hit over the fence will be judged fair or foul in respect to where the ball was when it passed over the fence, instead of where it landed. |
| 1926 | Ground-rule double if ball is batted over the fence in fair territory where the fence is less than 250 feet from home plate. |
| 1931 | A fair ball that bounces through or over a fence, or into the stands, is considered a ground-rule double instead of a home run. |
| 1950 | Strike zone to include only the area from the batter's armpits to the top of his knees. |
| 1959 | Professional fields constructed after June 1, 1958, must have a minimum distance of 325 feet on both the first and third base foul lines to the outfield fence, and a minimum of 400 feet to the center-field fence. |
| 1963 | Strike zone to include the area from the top of the shoulder to the bottom of the knee. |
| 1969 | Strike zone to include only the area from the armpit to the top of the knee. |
| 1987 | In early December, Commissioner Peter Ueberroth announced a further clarification of the strike zone. In a dissertation worthy of a Harvard law professor, Ueberroth announced that the upper limit of the strike zone would be the midpoint between the top of the shoulders and his pants—as the batter took his stance. The lower limit was the top of the knees. With both lines, the ball was supposed to be over the plate. |

Yeah, right, Pete.

# CAL RIPKEN JR.

KINGS OF SWING WHO MADE THE SLUGGERS SING

KINGS OF SWING WHO MADE THE SLUGGERS SING

KINGS OF SWING WHO MADE THE SLUGGERS SING

KINGS OF SWING WHO MADE THE SLUGGERS SING

KINGS OF SWING WHO MADE THE SLUGGERS SING

No one in the history of Major League Baseball has defined durability better than Cal Ripken Jr., who lugged a Louisville Slugger up to the plate in almost every one of the 2,131 games it took to break Lou Gehrig's record for most consecutive games played in before volunteering to take a day off in the 1999 season.

"I signed with Louisville Slugger right out of high school," he said. "With my dad being in baseball, I grew up around the game, and Louisville Slugger was the only option.

"Sure, there were other bats. But one of them stood up as well in terms of quality."

Ripken's father—Cal Ripken Sr., who coached and managed the Baltimore Orioles—had a large collection of bats in the family attic. Young Cal would go up there to play, picking through the models, became partial to thicker-handled bats at an early age.

Aluminum bats were becoming more popular when Ripken was playing Little League, but with his connections, Cal Ripken Sr. always ordered autographed wooden bats for his children: Cal Jr., Fred, Billy and Ellie.

"She was a great hitter," Cal Jr. said of his sister.

Ripken now swings a 35-inch, 33-ounce bat—and rarely changes during the season. He used the thicker-handled bat his first two years in professional baseball—and never hit a home run. Then, through a mistake in a shipping order, he received a batch of bats with thinner handles.

"I picked up a bat and it felt like a golf club might feel," he said. "That night I hit my first professional home run and I stayed with thinner handles ever since."

Ripken at Bat.
*Cal Ripken at bat in his familiar Orioles uniform.*

*T W O*

# THE SWEET
# SCIENCE
# OF HITTING

*BASEBALL PHYSICS FOR POETS*

The strong hands of Joe
DiMaggio show what's
required to hit a baseball.

In a sport dominated by statistics, the single most amazing fact in baseball is this: The meeting between the bat and ball, that brutal, violent, beautiful collision of white ash and cowhide, lasts about .001 second.

As in one one-thousandth of a second.

And the real damage is done in about half that time.

In less than the blink of an eye—well before the most nimble of appreciative fans can leap to their feet—an inbound, 95-mile-an-hour fastball is rocketing outbound at 120 miles an hour, the center fielder in hot pursuit, eyeing the ball nervously over his left shoulder.

The best of the center fielders are off before the crack of the bat, running on instinct and experience, their minds feeding their legs information; bat speed, pitch location, wind . . . warning track.

To best understand how a bat works, think about standing in place and swinging a weight on the end of a rope with two hands. The speed and power come at the far end of the rope, with little punch down near your hands.

In its simplest sense, the ball is a spring made of cork, yarn and cowhide. The bat compresses this spring. The ball pushes back against the bat, needing to regain its original round shape. The recoil pushes the ball toward the power alley, a blur of white rising against the expectant roar of the crowd.

The bat's arc will travel less than an inch while in contact with the ball. With as much as 8,000 pounds of pressure applied at impact, the baseball will be pancaked to about half its normal width, its appearance much more oval than round. The white ash of the bat has a give of only a few hundredths of an inch—if that.

There is good reason for the oft-repeated phrase: Hitting a baseball is the hardest thing to do in all of sports. A 90-mile-an-hour fastball will reach the plate in about four-tenths a second, but the pitch is almost halfway there before a batter can react.

The incredible ability to wait even a little longer on a pitch—literally until the last split second—is that very fine line that distinguishes the Hall of Fame hitters such as Joe DiMaggio from the players who never bat over .300, or never even get out of AA ball.

A great hitter's power—and bat speed—comes from his strong, quick wrists, incredible hand-eye coordination, and . . . practice, practice, practice. The "time of decision"—to swing or not to swing—is about 15-hundredths of a second. The batter must focus on the speed, rotation and direction of the pitch; fastball, slider, breaking ball or change-up. Is it going to be low and outside, breaking into his wrists or heading toward his chin?

Once the decision is made to swing, it takes about two-tenths of a second to do it. With the strongest and most supple of hitters, the tip of the bat might be moving at 80 to 90 miles an hour, while the handle is moving at less then 10 miles an hour. Hitting a major league baseball 500 feet generally requires that the ball be moving about 120 miles an hour as it leaves the bat.

For each 1.5 mph over 90 miles an hour, the ball is about a foot "quicker" to the plate, requiring constant adjustment for the hitter. If the swing is off by only seven-thousandths of a second, the result will be a swinging strike, a foul

**Impact of Baseball.**
*In only .001 of a second, a round baseball is flattened to almost pancake dimensions by the bat*

Concentration.
Johnny Bench demonstrates the
concentration that great hitters need.

ball or a weak dribbler to the infield. A swing an inch too low brings a towering pop-up; an inch too high, a ground ball to second.

Because they spend so much time behind the plate watching the balls come in—and too often go out—it would seem that catchers would have an advantage when they step to the plate to hit.

With rare exceptions, like Johnny Bench, who was catching for the Cincinnati Reds at age 19 and never looked back—that hasn't been the case. Bench was a great clutch hitter and a Gold Glove fielder, but few catchers have matched his numbers; the work involved behind the plate can keep your swing off by seven-thousandths of a second or so.

The science of hitting a baseball—the relationships among batter, bat and ball—is as interesting as the game. Those relationships, explained with the help of appropriate academic charts and graphs, have been well documented by Robert K. Adair, Yale University Sterling Professor of Physics, in his book *The Physics of Baseball.*

Adair wrote the book at the request of the late Bart Giamatti, who was president of Yale before moving on to become president of the National League and then commissioner of baseball. Giamatti gave Adair the title of "Physicist to the National League" for his work.

Adair dedicated his book to "the memory of my grandfather, Theodore Wiegman (1876-1953), who often sat with a small boy behind third base watching 3-I League baseball in the old Fort Wayne ball park in the 1930s, and to the memory of my son, James Cleland Adair (1957-1978), graceful first baseman on his championship Little League team."

Adair reminds us that official baseball rules allow bats to be "cupped"—altered with indentations in the end up to one inch deep and two inches wide, to lighten the swinging load.

t he rules also say the ball should be a sphere made of yarn wrapped around a smaller sphere of cork, rubber or similar material. It can't weigh less than 5 ounces or more than 5 $\frac{1}{4}$ ounces. It must be between 9 and 9 $\frac{1}{4}$ inches in circumference.

Going into further detail, a baseball's cork center is enclosed in rubber, which is wrapped with 121 yards of blue-gray wool yarn, 45 yards of white wool yarn and 150 yards of fine cotton yarn. If you're scoring at home, that's 316 yards of yarn—longer than three football fields—wrapped up inside a ball.

Hence the spring in the ball.

The core and 316 yards of yarn are then enclosed by rubber cement covered with two white pieces of cowhide (horsehide before 1974). The cover is hand-stitched together with precisely 216 red cotton stitches.

By hand. In Haiti.

That means baseball is one of the few games involving a ball, bat or club in which the ball is often the wider of the two. To get maximum results from hitting a ball, it must come in contact with the bat near a point the physicists call the "center of percussion"—but what your Little League coach always called the "sweet spot."

It's usually about six inches to eight inches from the end of the bat, but can move around, depending on where you hold a bat, or even the way you swing it. It is the point—and it is quite literally a point—where you get the biggest bang for your buck.

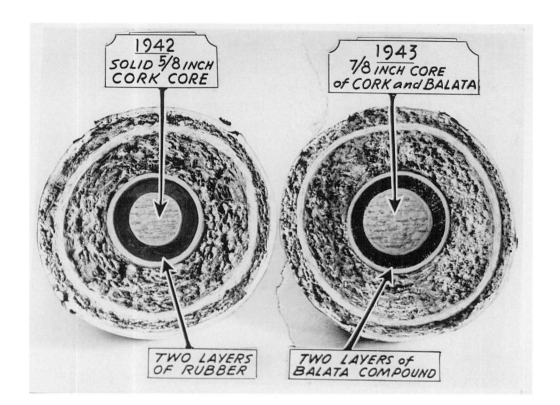

1942
SOLID 5/8 INCH
CORK CORE

1943
7/8 INCH CORE
of CORK and BALATA

TWO LAYERS
OF RUBBER

TWO LAYERS of
BALATA COMPOUND

**Inside the Seams.**
*Baseballs have evolved over the years, but it still takes more than 300 yards of yarn, cork, rubber and cowhide to make them fly.*

You can find the sweet spot on a bat by holding it a few inches below the knob with two fingers. Take a second bat and tap along the barrel of the bat you're holding. Work your way down the barrel until the bat you're holding stops vibrating. That's the sweet spot, the magic place where you can hit a baseball, barely feel the impact, and still "get it all."

That's important because a baseball returns only about 30 percent of the energy supplied when it is flattened by the bat. A golf ball, by comparison, returns more than 75 percent—which is why it goes farther. If a baseball were wound with rubber like a golf ball, the 400-foot home run would travel 600 feet.

The speed on an incoming pitch is a definite factor in how far the ball will fly when hit; a 90-mile-an-hour fastball will travel much farther than a 60-mile-an-hour curve when hit with the same bat swung at the same speed.

The wooden bat is actually more elastic than the baseball—hold that thought—but the bat is compressed much less on impact, so it supplies much less energy. If you don't believe that, try this trick: Drop a ball and a wooden bat from the same height onto a concrete floor. The bat will always bounce higher than the ball. And an aluminum bat will rebound higher than a wooden bat—which helps explain its hitting power and popularity.

When a hitter really lays into a pitch, about half the energy of the bat is transferred to the ball, thus slowing the bat speed by about 30 percent. And a lot of the bat/ball energy is lost in the frictional heat produced by the collision. The heat is no more than a few degrees, however, and the ball will cool down by the time you pick it up.

Years ago, Adair wrote, players used to hone their bats with hambones because they believed this would make the bat harder, and the ball would jump off it more quickly. Some would even hammer nails into the sweet spot area, hoping the ball would go farther. But since the bat stores so little energy on impact, hardening the bat serves no useful purpose

"Indeed," wrote Adair, "if the hitting area were armored with a thin sheet of absolutely hard and rigid steel, the well-hit ball would probably go slightly less far since energy would be lost as the distortion of the more elastic wood would be replaced by an increased distortion in the less elastic ball."

Baseball science has also shown that "corking" a bat by drilling a hole in its end, stuffing it with cork to make it lighter, then gluing the sawdust back over the hole may actually be counterproductive. Many a player has tried it—and been fined for it—but the very slight increase in bat speed is negated by the loss in bat mass.

There are so many physical factors involved in hitting a baseball for distance that sluggers probably couldn't get out of bed in the morning if they thought too much about it.

According to George Manning, vice president of technical services for Hillerich & Bradsby, a few of those factors include speed of the bat, speed of the ball, the mass of the ball, the location of the hit of the ball and the bat, the angle of the hit, the weather conditions, the ball's surface condition, the direction of the bat at impact, the direction of the ball at impact and—of course—the coefficient of restitution between bat and ball.

Or you can just get up there and swing.

What matters most is how fast you can swing the bat. Which explains why an average-sized guy like Henry Aaron—who did have incredibly strong, quick wrists—could hit 755 home runs.

"Because the mass of the bat is so much greater than the mass of the ball," Manning said, "bat velocity is a much more significant factor."

air resistance is also a factor; a batted ball that would travel 750 feet in a vacuum would travel only 400 feet if you wanted to breathe fresh air while watching it.

But air resistance is also very complex. The stitches on a baseball, which produce some air turbulence, actually help it fly farther in much the same way the dimples on a golf ball give it more distance in flight. The turbulence actually reduces the drag on a ball.

"Consequently," wrote Adair, "if the baseball were quite smooth rather than provided with stitches, it could not be thrown or batted nearly as far . . . A stitched baseball batted 400 feet would travel only about 300 feet if it were very smooth.

Baseballs spend a lot of time in the sky. A classic "mile high" pop-up will be in the air almost six seconds before settling in a shortstop's glove. A 385-foot fly ball batted at a 35-degree angle will be airborne for about five seconds.

If you bring into play even a 10-mile-an-hour wind blowing out—practically calm at Wrigley Field—a 370-foot fly ball will travel 400 feet. If you reverse the wind, take away the 30 feet, the 400-foot home run is another frustrating out on the warning track.

As any pitcher who has ever worked in Coors Field in Denver can tell you, altitude—which translates to air density—is also a big factor in fly balls.

Adair's statistics show that a 400-foot drive at sea level in Yankee Stadium would travel 407 feet in Atlanta—at an elevation of 1,050 feet. The same ball would travel about five feet farther in Kansas City, and 430 feet in Denver. In Mexico City—at an altitude of 7,800 feet—the same ball would travel 450 feet.

That subtle difference made it just a little more difficult for Roger Maris to hit his 61 home runs in 1961, although he also had the advantage of being a left-handed hitter in Yankee Stadium, which had a very short right-field foul line. But with Maris's quick bat, and by being in his prime, he was going to hit a lot of home runs for any team.

The thinner air at higher altitude does give a pitcher a tiny advantage; his fastball will be about six inches quicker in Denver than at sea level. On the other hand, his curveball will move about 25 percent less. A batted ball will also reach the 300-foot mark in the outfield "gap" about three-tenths of a second quicker in Denver, Adair warns, thus reducing the amount of time defenders have to react.

Temperature, barometric pressure and humidity also make a difference. A 400-foot drive will go about 20 feet farther on a 90-degree day than on a 45-degree day. A one-inch drop in barometric pressure will add 6 feet to the 400-foot shot. Contrary to public opinion—with water vapor actually being lighter than air—a baseball will travel farther on a very humid night, but only a few inches.

Still, there's nothing better than a warm night at the ol' ballpark.

**Home Run Slugging.**
*Roger Maris set the modern home run record years before Sammy Sosa and Mark McGwire.*

# KIRBY PUCKETT

*KINGS OF SWING WHO MADE THE SLUGGERS SING*

*KINGS OF SWING WHO MADE THE SLUGGERS SING*

*KINGS OF SWING WHO MADE THE SLUGGERS SING*

*KINGS OF SWING WHO MADE THE SLUGGERS SING*

*KINGS OF SWING WHO MADE THE SLUGGERS SING*

Growing up as the youngest of nine children in a Chicago housing project, Kirby Puckett found his choice of hitting equipment pretty much defined by the neighborhood.

"As a kid, I never remembered what I used," he said. "We used what was available."

With his father working two jobs to take care of his family, whatever was available included old bats and balls made from socks and aluminum foil. By the time he got to high school, his choice in bats was mostly the Louisville Slugger.

When his father died in 1981, Puckett was going to quit school to help his family, but his mother, who had always stayed home to take care of her children, wouldn't allow it. She saw a future in baseball for her son and encouraged him to continue with school—and baseball.

"I first signed professionally in 1982," he said. "Louisville Slugger signed me to a contract in 1984. I used their bats exclusively after that. I never used anything else."

Puckett batted .296 for the Minnesota Twins in 1984 and was named Rookie of the Year. At 5 feet 8 and 215 pounds, he was not a prototypical center fielder—or hitter—but he led the league in hits four times and won the batting title with a .339 average in 1989. He also led the Twins to World Series championships in 1987 and 1991 with Louisville Slugger bats. For most of those years, he used a 34 $\frac{1}{2}$-inch, 33-ounce bat, but he always trusted Hillerich & Bradsby to take care of him.

"It's not the bow," he said. "It's the Indian that's shooting it. I liked the product. The company always took care of me. I got 2,300 hits in 12 years. I got no complaints."

In 1996, after batting .314 and .317 the previous two years, Puckett learned he had glaucoma. After five unsuccessful operations, he had to retire. He was a lifetime .318 hitter and had a .989 fielding average, committing an average of only four errors a year.

A Twin.
*Kirby Puckett*

T H R E E

# BIG BAT, BIG STORY

*HOW THE LOUISVILLE SLUGGER BECAME*
*THE BAT OF THE BIG LEAGUES*

Ty Cobb.
*In 1908, Ty Cobb, still holding baseball's best lifetime batting average, agreed to endorse bats for J.F. Hillerich & Son.*

t he story of the most famous label in baseball history, the Louisville Slugger, began in the 1880s with Hillerich-family tradition, swinging butter churns and a single baseball bat—created pretty much as an afterthought.

Over the next 115 years—and millions of bats—Louisville Sluggers would be swung by the greatest players in history: Honus Wagner, Ty Cobb, Babe Ruth, Lou Gehrig, Ted Williams, Jackie Robinson, Joe DiMaggio, Stan Musial, Mickey Mantle, Henry Aaron, Roberto Clemente, Pete Rose, George Brett, Tony Gwynn, Alex Rodriguez, Ken Griffey Jr., Derek Jeter and Sammy Sosa.

The Hillerich name and ownership—now into its fifth generation—is as robust and prominent as ever. But this family baseball story must be taken one base at a time.

The Hillerich family tradition actually dates from 1842, when J. Michael Hillerich brought his family from Baden-Baden, Germany, to Baltimore, then on to Louisville. At that time it was a booming city of more than 20,000 people, the twelfth-largest in the nation.

The Hillerichs had long worked with their hands, fashioning wood into barrels, ax handles, plows, bed posts and handrails. Louisville, at the time, was considered "the West," a natural stopping place for Ohio River traffic that fed the nation's interior. Travelers included fortune hunters headed west for the California Gold Rush. Neither baseball—nor any game close to it—was much on the mind of these early pioneers.

By 1850, Louisville had more than 40,000 residents, many of them needing Hillerich's wood products. In 1859, after apprenticing with his immigrant father, John Frederich Hillerich opened his own woodshop and barrel-making business in a two-story brick building at 22 Clay Street near the busy Ohio River in downtown Louisville.

He called his firm "J.F. Hillerich, Job Turning." It shared space with the Clay Street Planing Mill, a squat, two-story red-brick building advertised as a "Door, Blind, Sash & Box Factory." Early photographs of the factory showed half a dozen men leaning out windows that also served as loading areas; teams of horses and wagons waited on the dirt street below to deliver raw lumber.

Baseball—often then called Base Ball—was in its Kentucky infancy, a game for "gentlemen" played with crude balls and bats and a mishmash of rules. Yet its ability to stir fan interest was apparent from the first pitch.

The first well-publicized game in Louisville took place on July 19, 1865, when a quickly organized team from Louisville's high society whipped a team from Nashville 22-5. The pitcher, one "Captain Booth," tossed the ball underhand to a catcher who was described as being "under the bat," although he stood 20 feet behind the plate.

The game was well covered by the press because of the business rivalry between the towns. News accounts indicated the 200 fans were nicely entertained, but many didn't have a clue about what they were watching.

By 1875, J.F. Hillerich's woodworking business was doing so well, he moved it to 118 S. First Street between Main and Market streets. The location,

**The Beginning.**
*J. Frederich Hillerich opened his woodshop in Louisville in 1859.*

*Crack of the Bat: The Louisville Slugger Story*

incidentally, was only seven downtown blocks from the place where the $14 million Louisville Slugger Museum, factory and office complex would open 121 years later.

In the 1870s, Louisville's population would surpass 100,000. It was considered, along with Chicago, St. Louis and Cincinnati, one of the country's great interior cities. Paddlewheelers, flatboats and barges carrying cotton, cast-iron pipe and passengers tied up along the city's cobblestone wharf.

J.F. Hillerich's nearby shop supplied the growing city's steady demand for porch columns and stair railings, as well as its sports community's need for tenpins, duckpins and wooden bowling balls.

The workers were old-world craftsmen, standing for hours before wood lathes driven by belts and powered by boilers fired from the shavings. Given a porch rail, duckpin or bowling ball as a model, the workers could easily duplicate it with their razor-sharp tools, occasionally checking their work with calipers, rubbing strong hands over the smooth, clean wood.

By 1876, baseball—especially professional baseball—had taken a toehold in the city; Louisville became a charter member of the newly formed Na-

**Old Hickory.**
*Horse-drawn wagons hauled the bats in the early days.*

tional League. In its infancy, the league was poorly funded and little respected, although its commissioner, William Hulbert, did try to give it some credence by banning alcohol, gambling and Sunday games.

The bans were much needed. Baseball had moved quickly—maybe too quickly—from amateur to professional ranks. By the 1860s, professional teams had been formed in New York, Washington, Chicago, Pittsburgh, Philadelphia, Baltimore and Cincinnati, the latter a team so strong, it took historical claim as the country's first professional team—although it wasn't.

Professional baseball was quickly riddled with corruption, bad contracts and players selling out to gamblers. In 1877, Louisville's front-running entry in the National League—the Louisville Grays—did little to elevate the league's image, as four players were banned for life after admitting to fixing games. "The Louisville Four" gave professional baseball a major league scandal, and Louisville dropped out of the National League.

It was three years later—in 1880—when J.F. Hillerich's son, John A. "Bud" Hillerich, began his apprenticeship in his father's First Street shop. Bud Hillerich was only 14 years old. But he had completed grade school, which was all the education most boys were given in those days, and it was time for him to go to work.

By the time of his death in 1946, Bud Hillerich would be credited with changing the way a baseball-crazy nation, and the world, talked and thought about bats—"Louisville Slugger" bats.

the story of the Hillerich family's first bat has become clouded in myth, memory and baseball lore, but there's no doubt it was turned in J.F. Hillerich's shop, and that his young son, Bud, had his hands in on it.

The most enduring and appealing first-bat story involves another Louisville legend, Louis Rogers "Pete" Browning and his team, the Louisville Eclipse. After the city's fall from baseball grace with the "Louisville Four," Louisville climbed back into professional baseball in 1882, becoming a charter member of a new major league, the American Association.

The unabashed star of that team was Browning, nicknamed "The Gladiator." Even if his lifetime .341 average over 13 years didn't get him into the Hall of Fame, his talent—and idiosyncrasies—made him a celebrity and a curiosity. The screwball wasn't named for Browning, but it might have been.

Browning was born in Louisville, but never attended school: he was partially deaf and had difficulty learning. He was a city marbles champion and a natural baseball player. His teammates included Toad Ramsey, Lave Cross and a man with the most memorable name in baseball history, Chicken Wolf.

Browning became a legend. He often refused to slide into a base; he would catch a ball standing on one leg; he kept track of his hits on the cuff of his shirt; and he spoke to everyone in a booming, quirky voice because he could not hear himself speak. He also had a legendary drinking problem—he called beer "German Tea"—which magnified all his other traits.

But Browning also was remembered for being one of the first players who cared about his bats, taking many of them home to his basement late in

"The Old Gladiator"
PETE BROWNING. Left Field

The Old Gladiator.
*Legend has it, the always entertaining*
*Pete Browning may have ordered the first*
*Louisville Slugger.*

his career, apparently believing there were no more hits left in them. He would personalize his bats, giving them names like Mary, Joe, Kate and Lazarus, the latter apparently a bat of some durability.

Browning played at Eclipse Park at 28th and Elliott streets in Louisville. According to the most prevalent first-bat legend, 17-year-old J.A. "Bud" Hillerich had slipped away from his father's shop one afternoon in 1884 to watch a game. When the boy saw Browning—then in the midst of a slump—break a bat, he went over to him, tugged at his sleeve and offered to make him a new one.

After the game, Browning, and Hillerich went to the First Street shop, where Hillerich—with Browning constantly offering advice—hand-turned a new bat. Browning pounded out three hits the next day, then spread the word to his Eclipse teammates, who began beating a path to Bud Hillerich's lathe.

Baseball historian and former Louisvillian Bob Bailey, writing an article for the Society for American Baseball Research (SABR), noted another first-bat story. This story suggests that young Bud Hillerich was actually a fine baseball player himself on a neighborhood team, and that his father made the first bat for him, but declared himself entirely too busy to make another. But when Bud's teammates—especially a pitcher named Gus Weyhing—saw the

quality of the bat, they prevailed on the elder Hillerich to make more. A variation of that tale was that young Bud first made his own bats; who better to do it?

Yet another story was given life in a 1937 *Baseball* magazine article. It said a loquacious old-timer named Arlie Latham, nicknamed "The Freshest Man on Earth," claimed J.F. Hillerich turned the company's first bat for him in 1883 or 1884. But then—in addition to freshness—hyperbole was one of Latham's finest attributes.

Pete Browning was mentioned in a lengthy 1914 interview with J.F. Hillerich published in the *Louisville Herald* magazine—but in a different context. In that story, Hillerich said Browning had been in a slump and had come to the First Street shop on his own for help—a bat already in hand.

"I can't hit a thing with it," Browning supposedly said to Hillerich.

"Well . . . I'll put a home run in it for you," offered Hillerich.

"Mr. Hillerich took the bat, put it in a lathe, and scratched a circle around it. That afternoon Pete poled the promised homer, and ever afterwards his bats were made with rings around them."

If Hillerich made the first bat for Browning—or even put a ring around his bat—it was never mentioned by the effervescent Browning in any of the

**Eclipse Team.**
*The Louisville Eclipse team was part of the American Association—then part of the major leagues.*

*Crack of the Bat: The Louisville Slugger Story*

many stories written about him, or in his lengthy obituary. So linking him to the first bat may have evolved from a melding of the several stories, especially the one about the ring around his bat.

What is certain is that the firm could turn a good bat, the Eclipse team needed the product and, by the early 1880s, the Hillerichs found themselves in the bat business, with word of their ability spreading from team to team as they came through Louisville.

At first the Hillerichs just made a variety of standard bats; the players chose from them. The Hillerichs quickly learned the secret of their success would be to find out exactly what a player wanted—and make it—a tradition that continues today.

The irony was that in the 1880s, J.F. Hillerich was not looking for baseball business. In fact, as the 1914 *Louisville Herald* story indicates, he didn't even want it.

"Mr. Hillerich could not dodge the demand," the story said. "The more he made, the more he was requested to make, much to his displeasure.

"And there was a reasonable objection, because the compensation was not equivalent to the time essential to turn a well-balanced bat. It was a losing proposition and the swatters who continued to come seeking sticks were considered a nuisance, second to none.

Their persistence irritated Mr. Hillerich, and for a time the doors were barred against the uniform union."

What changed the equation was that Bud Hillerich hurt his shoulder in a fall, ending his baseball career, but giving him more time to make bats for others.

"Young Hillerich saw the possibilities of a big bat business," the article said, "and his father was so pleased with the enthusiasm that Bud displayed in the idea that he gave his consent to the project and they lost no time in forming the foundation for the Louisville Slugger success."

There had been another roadblock in the Louisville Slugger's path: swinging butter churns. By the late 1880s, the company had become J.F. Hillerich & Son, Wood Turners, Band and Scroll Sawing. A strong product in its wood arsenal was a swinging butter churn, which had been patented by a William H. Curtice of Eminence, Kentucky. The "Creamery Swing Churn" was built

**Eclipse Park.**
*The Eclipse team played in Eclipse Park in Louisville in the 1880s.*

# TONY GWYNN

*KINGS OF SWING WHO MADE THE SLUGGERS SING*

*KINGS OF SWING WHO MADE THE SLUGGERS SING*

*KINGS OF SWING WHO MADE THE SLUGGERS SING*

*KINGS OF SWING WHO MADE THE SLUGGERS SING*

*KINGS OF SWING WHO MADE THE SLUGGERS SING*

Batting tees would seem to belong in the world of small children playing T-ball before bleachers full of adoring/screaming parents, but perennial National League batting champion Tony Gwynn of the San Diego Padres works on his game from a tee, too.

"During January I will hit 50 balls a day off a batting tee," Gwynn said in his foreword to *The Louisville Slugger Ultimate Book of Hitting.*

"Hitting off a batting tee is the best way to perfect your swing, the surest path to developing consistent form and to learning to hit to all fields."

Gywnn was San Diego's third-round draft choice in June 1981. He signed with Hillerich & Bradsby that year while still in the Instructional League and has swung a Louisville Slugger ever since—now using a 32 $\frac{1}{2}$ in., 31 oz. model.

"I'm old enough I grew up hitting with a wooden bat," said Gwynn. "A Willie Davis model.

"I signed with the company in about a half-hour, and when I got to the big leagues I got my bat, and it had my signature on it. It was a lousy signature, but it was a Louisville Slugger and I felt like I had arrived.

"You shoot yourself in the foot if you don't go up to the plate with a bat you're comfortable with."

Shooting is also something Gwynn could do with proficiency; he was a good enough basketball player to become a draft choice of the NBA's San Diego Clippers. That he ultimately chose the right sport, however, became apparent long before Gwynn joined one of baseball's most exclusive clubs when he reached the 3,000-hit milestone in 1999.

A Proud Padre.
*Tony Gwynn*

Louisville Base Ball Club.
*This casual pose of The Louisville Base Ball Club was typical of the 1880s.*

The Second Generation.
*Bud Hillerich was the first man to see the business possibilities in producing baseball bats.*

on a frame, which meant the raw milk could be rocked rather than beaten with a plunger. It came with a special attachment that would allow mothers to rock their babies at the same time.

The churn was so popular that J.F. Hillerich did not want to take time away from its production—and his other products—to fool with baseball bats. With its scandals and eternal folding of professional leagues, the game did not enjoy a wholesome reputation anyway. But an 1895 advertisement indicated the company found a way to swing both bats and butter. It read: "This business was established by Mr. J.F. Hillerich and conducted by him alone until he took his son Mr. J.A. Hillerich in partnership, since which time the affairs of the company have passed more and more into the hands of the son, who now practically manages the business.

"The premises occupied comprise a two-storied brick building 26 x 135 feet in dimensions, fully equipped with the latest improved appliances and machinery for woodworking.

"They are also the manufacturers of the dairy swing churn, which is unquestionably the best, cheapest and most durable churn that has yet been put in the market, and they also manufacture baseball bats, which have secured a national reputation for efficiency, strength and finish . . . From fifteen to twenty skilled hands are employed, and nothing but the very best work is ever turned out."

*Crack of the Bat: The Louisville Slugger Story*

## LOUISVILLE OF TO-DAY

J. F. HILLERICH & SON; Wood Turners, Band and Scroll Sawing, Etc.; No. 216 First Street.—In reviewing the industries of this enterprising city, we find several houses which, owing to their many years of existence and the superiority of their productions deserve especially prominent mention. Such a concern is that of Messrs. J. F. Hillerich & Son, wood turners and woodworkers. This business was established in 1865 by Mr. J. F. Hillerich and conducted by him alone until the year 1888, when he took his son Mr. J. A. Hillerich in partnership, since which time the affairs of the company have passed more and more into the hands of the son, who now practically manages the business. The premises occupied comprise a two-storied brick building 26x135 feet in dimensions, fully equipped with the latest improved appliances and machinery for woodworking, in addition to band and scroll sawing of all kinds. They manufacture every description of bored porch columns, newel posts, brackets and poles, also manufacture fancy woodwork for interior and exterior decoration of buildings. They are also the manufacturers of the dairy swing churn, which is unquestionably the best, cheapest and most durable churn that has yet been put in the market, and they also manufacture baseball bats, which have secured a national reputation for efficiency, strength and finish. From fifteen to twenty skilled hands are employed, and nothing but the very best work is ever turned out, perfect satisfaction as regards quality of materials and workmanship being fully guaranteed. Mr. Hellerich, senior, was born in Germany, but has made his home in Louisville for many years. Mr. J. A. Hellerich, the son, has long been known for business capacity and skilled ability. He was born in this city, and has gained the confidence of the firm's numerous customers.

ISSUED BY THE
CONSOLIDATED ILLUSTRATING COMPANY,
LOUISVILLE, KY.
1895.

**Bat and churn.**
*In a great compromise, this 1895 J. F. Hillerich & Son ad featured bats and swinging butter churns.*

**Churn.**
*Before baseball bats, J.F. Hillerich believed the company's future lay in swinging butter churns.*

A famous photograph of that shop showed nine of those skilled hands gathered in a casual row at its front door, staring into the camera, if not history. Four of them, including Bud Hillerich, were holding bats. The other five, including his bearded father, were not.

By any vote imaginable, that was about the last time baseball would be an also-ran to a swinging churn. By the 1880s, big sporting-goods wholesalers developed to expedite sales to far-flung retail stores. In 1890 J.F. Hillerich signed an agreement with the Simmons Hardware Company of St. Louis to handle all its bat sales, except for those to professional baseball players and a few chosen outlets.

At first, their bats had been called the "Hillerich" bats, then the "Falls City Slugger"—so labeled because of Louisville's proximity to the Falls of the Ohio, a long series of Ohio River rapids at its side door.

**Roots.**

*This famous photo of the employees of "The World's First Bat Factory" was taken in the late 1800s, when the wood mill was on First Street in downtown Louisville. The two men at the extreme left are Henry Bickel, who worked with the company for 60 years, and J. Fred Hillerich (in the beard), the company founder. His son, J. A. "Bud" Hillerich, who may have turned the first bat for the company, is standing in the doorway, holding a bat.*

No one person has been credited with changing the bat's name to the "Louisville Slugger." The best theory is that the players who used the bat created the name. Whatever the case, in 1894 the name "Louisville Slugger" was registered in the U.S. Patent Office under certificate No. 50,812. It would soon grow in sports context well beyond any city; it would come to symbolize an entire game.

In 1897 the firm would become J.F. Hillerich & Son. The partnership included the sale of one-half of the First Street lot owned by John F. Hillerich and his wife, Ella, to their son, John A. "Bud" Hillerich, then 31. The 1897 sales agreement indicated that an interesting financial situation had developed between father and son:

"THAT WHEREAS J.F. HILLERICH AND JOHN A. HILLERICH HAVE BEEN ENGAGED IN BUSINESS FOR A NUMBER OF YEARS AND THE PROPERTY HEREINAFTER DESCRIBED IS PART OF THE ASSETS OF SAID BUSINESS; AND WHEREAS SAID PARTY J.F. HILLERICH IS LARGELY OVERDRAWN IN HIS ACCOUNT WITH THE SAID FIRM; AND WHEREAS SAID SECOND PARTY HAS BOARDED WITH SAID FIRST PARTIES, WHO ARE HIS MOTHER AND FATHER,

SINCE HE ARRIVED AT AGE TWENTY-ONE YEARS, AND HAS NOT PAID ANY
BOARD DURING SAID PERIOD, AND IT IS AGREED BY BOTH PARTIES THAT
ALL INDEBTEDNESS BETWEEN THEM IS HEREBY SATISFIED AND CANCELLED
IN FULL TO THIS DATE OF CONVEYANCE."

The half interest in the building, according to that contract, was then
sold for $1 "cash."

By the late 1890s, the Louisville Slugger trademark appeared on bats
used by many of the game's early stars, including Wee Willie Keeler, Pete
Browning, Hugh Duffy, John McGraw and the five Delahanty brothers. Their
names were branded on the bat in block lettering—an improvement over the
tradition of players carving their initials on the knob or barrel of the bat for
identification purposes.

By 1901, J.F. Hillerich & Son had more bat business than room to turn
the bats, so the operation was moved to another old building in Louisville, a

**Bat Factory.**
*This 1912 photo of the J.F.
Hillerich & Son factory
shows its prime product
proudly advertised.*

two-story, Civil War-era structure at 729 S. Preston Street between Finzer and Jacob streets. The company would stay there for more than 70 years.

J.F. Hillerich—Bud's father—remained in the First Street shop—which served as the office for both businesses, where he continued to make swinging churns and porch rails for Louisville's Victorian houses. He retired in 1916, at age 82. In 1924, still an active 90, he slipped on an icy Louisville street, caught pneumonia during his recovery and died.

Meanwhile, Bud Hillerich's bat business continued to grow into the 1900s. A 1912 photograph showed the 729 S. Preston Street shop to be another squat, brick building—but with an attitude. This one had an advertising message written across its front: "J.F. HILLERICH & SON CO.—Sole MANU-FACTURERS of the CELEBRATED 'LOUISVILLE SLUGGER' BAT."

A *Sporting Goods Dealer* magazine article called the structure the "largest, oldest and only exclusive base ball bat factory in the world"—with base ball still being spelled as two words. The story went on in some romantic detail about the "lanky mountaineers from Kentucky" felling the second-growth ash timber and hauling it 30 miles to sawmills.

**t**he wood had to be shipped to Louisville and dried for at least a year. Once "roughed out" on a lathe to determine its general condition, only about one piece of wood in 10 had enough good grain to qualify as a professional bat.

The remaining wood was used for the company's other bats. Its machines were turning out 2,000 bats a day for general use, but the men who hand-turned the bats for professional players produced about 35 a day.

Hillerich said at the time he preferred Kentucky wood, and only ash could be used—with the exception of majaqua, a Cuban-grown wood that the Hillerichs turned just for Cuban players. The Cuban bats sold for $2; all other professional level bats sold for about $1.50.

The company had to deal with thousands of individual bat sizes requested by ballplayers. In time, each player had his own "card," which noted the dimensions of the bats he preferred. It was a system that, in general, would change very little for about 100 years, although bat records are now stored on company computers.

What did change in baseball—and eventually in all sports—was the marketing. That became a brand-new ball game on Sept. 1, 1905: Honus Wagner, the "Flying Dutchman," who had 3,418 hits and batted .327 over 21 seasons with Louisville and Pittsburgh, signed a contract giving J.F. Hillerich & Son permission to use his autograph on Louisville Slugger bats.

This "endorsement advertising" was the first of its kind. It quickly became another company trademark—linking the product with the men who best used it. The practice continued well into the modern baseball era, eventually giving us the universally recognized Michael Jordan and the Nike swoosh. The company would eventually sign more than 7,000 men to contracts—most of whom never saw a major league pitch.

Wagner's endorsement was quickly followed by one from Napoleon "Nap" Lajoie, whose .422 batting average in 1901 set an American League

**Bat Cards.**
*Way before computers, the dimensions of a player's favorite bat were kept on individual cards.*

Honus Wagner.
In 1905 Honus Wagner changed sports marketing forever by contracting to allow J. F. Hillerich & Son to put his name on a bat.

record that still stands. But J.F. Hillerich & Son's biggest coup would come in October 1908, when the mercurial Ty Cobb signed a contract. Cobb, obsessed, fiery and both revered and hated, still holds the record for the highest lifetime batting average—a robust .367—and his name would sell a lot of bats.

J.A. "Bud" Hillerich—with only a grade school education but an ingrained genius for creating tools and equipment—would spend a lifetime in pursuit of better bats and other items. In the 1920s he was granted patents for bowling pins, golf club heads and better ways to laminate wood strips. He worked for years on Hillerich & Bradsby's "powerizing process"—a way to force liquid cement into wood grain to keep a bat from chipping. He designed many of the machines used to shape and sand his bats.

To stay competitive in the late 1800s and early 1900s, Hillerich & Son was producing thousands of less-expensive "brand name" bats for chain stores and mail-order houses such as Montgomery Ward.

Its biggest seller was a "Buster Brown" bat, which in 1907 accounted for about 75 percent of all company bat sales (which totaled about $17,000, according to a story on the company in the 1993 *Sports Marketing Quarterly*). But in 1907 the company was selling the "Buster Brown" bats wholesale for 30 cents a dozen. Retail customers could buy one for a dime—or even a nickel.

Hillerich could advertise names such as Wagner, Lajoie, Cobb and, later, Frank "Home Run" Baker. In the era of the "dead ball," Baker led the American League in home runs four years in a row (1911-14) without hitting more than 12. Baker became a national celebrity when he hit consecutive game-winning home runs off Hall of Fame pitchers Rube Marquard and Christy Mathewson in the 1911 World Series.

Those names helped sell the more expensive, top-grade "Louisville Slugger" models, but in the early 1900s, Hillerich & Son was still just one of about two dozen small, struggling companies producing bats in the United States. Not one of the others born in that era would survive.

# BASEBALL BAT FACTORY IS GUTTED BY FLAMES

## J. F. Hillerich & Son Suffer $50,000 Loss In Fire That Raged Eight Hours.

*Up in Flames. A fire destroyed much of the factory in 1910.*

Work in the old Hillerich factory was very much a hands-on, turn-of-the-century endeavor. The environment was red-brick walls, wooden floors and exposed beams. Employees—men and teenaged boys—worked in dim, hot, dusty, crowded factory aisles littered with wood shavings. The bats were moved about on old, steel-wheeled dollies between lathes and sanders driven by long belts.

"In the olden days," said a story in the *Sporting Goods Dealer*, "the players would often take with them to the factory a piece of wagon tongue or a section of tree they had seasoned themselves. They would give instructions to the turner and then they would wait until the bat was finished."

Air-dried ash—and in the early days, some hickory—was stacked in company timber yards in immense rows about 40 feet high and hundreds of feet long. Each row had to be restacked three times a year to facilitate drying and to keep insects from chewing the raw lumber.

The danger of fire was constant, and on Dec. 14, 1910, a headline in a Louisville newspaper screamed the almost inevitable:

BASEBALL BAT FACTORY IS GUTTED BY FLAMES
J.F. Hillerich & Son Suffer $50,000 Loss
In Fire That Raged Eight Hours

The fire—of undetermined cause—was discovered by a fireman on watch at No. 9 Engine Company a short distance away. The newspaper account

# GEORGE BRETT

*KINGS OF SWING WHO MADE THE SLUGGERS SING*

*KINGS OF SWING WHO MADE THE SLUGGERS SING*

*KINGS OF SWING WHO MADE THE SLUGGERS SING*

*KINGS OF SWING WHO MADE THE SLUGGERS SING*

*KINGS OF SWING WHO MADE THE SLUGGERS SING*

Few "flashback memories" in major league history will top a somewhat exercised George Brett storming from his Kansas City dugout on July 24, 1983, to protest an umpire's decision in the famous—or infamous—"Pine Tar" incident.

Brett had hit a ninth-inning home run against the Yankees, but the umpire had disallowed it—and given the victory to the Yankees—after Yankee manager Billy Martin complained that Brett had more than the allowable 18 inches of pine tar on the bat. Any more tar than that, and the ball often gets coated.

Brett, a .305 lifetime hitter with 3,154 hits, would get into the Hall of Fame anyway. He is the only player in major league history to win a batting title in three different decades—in 1976, 1980 and 1990.

American League president Lee MacPhail would overrule the original pine-tar decision. He ordered the game continued with Kansas City ahead on August 18, and the Royals won in 12 minutes.

Brett had used a Louisville Slugger his entire career, and Hillerich & Bradsby commemorated the event by selling nationwide a "Pine Tar Special" bat—complete with pine tar—to interested fans. It also produced a mini-bat—complete with pine tar.

In July 1996, 13 years later, Brett came to Louisville as one of a dozen Hall of Fame ballplayers who attended the opening of the Louisville Slugger Museum.

"I got a chance to finally meet Ted Williams for the first time," Brett said at the time. "But I was just honored to be here, to be invited by Louisville."

Royalty.
*George Brett takes a swing.*

said the brick building—built in 1864—"burned like paper" due to the flammable materials used to preserve the wood.

The second floor was destroyed, but much of the first-floor machinery was saved, as were the models of the bats used by the players, giving the workers replicas from which to turn new ones. All the firm's books were saved; they had remained at the old First Street office.

The stacks of billets stored outside the Preston Street factory also were saved by the resolute firemen, who became coated with ice during the eight-hour struggle in freezing temperatures. Firemen working their way through the gutted building had to hurl burning and charred bats out windows as they went, covering the street below with the smoking debris. The fire struck at a bad time; the company was preparing for its spring shipment of bats.

"I have not considered the question of rebuilding, and cannot say at present what our plans will be," J.A. "Bud" Hillerich said. "We employed between 40 and 50 men, and some of them will be thrown out of work temporarily."

If an ad that ran in the March 1911 *Sporting Goods Dealer* is any indication, the company's competitors lost no time in using the fire against them, even as it immediately began rebuilding:

> NOTICE TO THE TRADE:
> AS SOME OF OUR COMPETITORS HAVE CIRCULATED THE REPORT THAT OUR PLANT WAS TOTALLY DESTROYED BY OUR RECENT FIRE AND THAT WE WOULD NOT REBUILD. WE WISH TO STATE THAT WE ARE NOW RUNNING WITH A LARGER CAPACITY THAN EVER, AND THAT OUR STOCK OF SEASONED MATERIAL IS LARGER THAN ALL OTHER FACTORIES COMBINED. WE ALSO WISH TO WARN THE PUBLIC THAT SOME MANUFACTURERS ARE USING THE NAMES AND INITIALS COBB, LAJOIE, COLLINS, WAGNER, AND SLUGGER BATS. THIS IS AN INFRINGEMENT ON OUR TRADE MARK AND WE WILL PROTECT SAME TO FULL EXTENT OF LAW.

appearing next to the warning was a photo of Ty Cobb praising the Slugger bats, giving exclusive right to use his name and placing an order for another dozen autographed models—from 44 to 46 ounces in weight.

Financial salvation for the Hillerichs—and an eventual change in the company name—came in the presence of Frank W. Bradsby, who in 1911 would add his marketing genius to the Hillerich product. By 1923—in just 12 years—the "Hillerich & Bradsby Company" would be the biggest seller of bats in the country.

Bradsby was born in Lebanon, Illinois, in 1878, moving to St. Louis with his family in 1885. He quit high school at 15 to go to work for the Simmons Hardware Company, the largest hardware house in the world, because he was so eager to get started in business.

At 20 he quit Simmons to enlist in the U.S. Army to fight in the Spanish-American War. When he returned to Simmons, he advanced quickly, working as a traveling salesman, selling fishing tackle and guns and ammunition and then taking over the sales of all its athletic equipment. He was an energetic, confident, well-groomed man who would grow to love deep-sea fishing and horse racing; he would own a horse named Louisville Slugger. With Simmons, he traveled the country in his job, meeting with manufacturers and other salespeople. He frequently met with J.F. Hillerich and his son, Bud, to discuss their Louisville Slugger bats. For Simmons, Bradsby negotiated exclusive distribution rights for the Louisville Sluggers.

The elder Hillerich respected Bradsby so much that he began asking him to come to Louisville to discuss specific business problems. In 1911, after the fire had devastated the firm, Bradsby, 33, moved to Louisville to stamp his name and sales expertise on the company.

Some of the fire loss had been covered by insurance, but the Hillerichs needed capital, and Bradsby, along with several members of his family, would buy stock in a reorganized company.

To set the stage, J.F. Hillerich & Son was incorporated as the J.F. Hillerich and Son Company. Then Bradsby—according to an article in the *Sporting Goods Dealer*—bought the business from J.F. Hillerich after his son Bud had sold his interest to his father. Bradsby would later reorganize the firm, with Bud Hillerich as president. Bradsby was secretary and treasurer, but with controlling interest.

According to Hillerich family lore, the business intrigue in that sale ran deep. The story goes that J.F. Hillerich no longer wanted Bud in the bat business, so Bud and Bradsby prearranged the deal to allow Bradsby to buy the firm, then to bring Bud back into it. Bradsby was a marketer, but he knew he had to have Bud Hillerich in the business if he wanted to keep producing bats.

A bill of sale dated July 10, 1911, between J.F. Hillerich and F.W. Bradsby, stated:

> THAT IN CONSIDERATION OF THE SUM OF ONE HUNDRED AND TWENTY-FIVE THOUSAND ($125,000), CASH IN HAND PAID, THE RECEIPT WHEREOF I NOW ACKNOWLEDGE, I (J.F. HILLERICH) HEREBY SELL, GRANT AND CONVEY UNTO THE SAID F.W. BRADSBY ALL THE MACHINERY, FIXTURES, RAW MATERIAL, MANUFACTURED ARTICLES, STOCKS OF GOODS, COPY RIGHTS, TRADE NAMES, TRADE MARKS, GOOD WILL AND ALL OTHER ITEMS PERTAINING TO OR CONNECTED WITH THE BASEBALL BAT BUSINESS HERETOFORE CONDUCTED BY J.F. HILLERICH & SON AT PRESTON AND JACOB STREET, LOUISVILLE, KENTUCKY.

Even after this contract had been ironed out, the deal still was not settled. In February of 1912, Bradsby had to fire off an angry letter to J.F. Hillerich, who was refusing to turn over "the Trade Mark papers which were included in the bill of sale dated July 10, 1911 . . . "

The deal was finally settled. In 1916, the firm's name was changed to the Hillerich & Bradsby Company.

By the time Bradsby bought controlling interest in the company, baseball was a national passion. On the National League's opening day in 1910,

**Frank Bradsby.**
*It was Frank Bradsby's business sense combined with the Hillerich expertise that would build the Hillerich & Bradsby Company into the world's foremost maker of bats.*

**Eclipse Park.**
*This standing-room-only crowd in Louisville's Eclipse Park in 1914 shows how baseball dominated the country's interest.*

President William Howard Taft—all 300-plus pounds of him—became the first president in history to throw out the first pitch. It was caught by Walter "Big Train" Johnson of the Washington Senators. He promptly threw a one-hitter at the Philadelphia Athletics.

The hitting stars of the 1910-20 era were Ty Cobb, Nap Lajoie, Tris Speaker, "Shoeless" Joe Jackson of the infamous 1919 Chicago "Black Sox" and a young slugger named George Herman "Babe" Ruth. He hit 11 home runs for the Boston Red Sox in 1918, then 29 in 1919. The next year, he hit an astounding 54 home runs for the New York Yankees. All those hitters used Louisville Sluggers.

Bradsby's sales vision drove the company to similar heights. According to a 1993 article in *Sports Marketing Quarterly* authored by three University of Louisville professors—Lori Miller, Lawrence Fielding and Brenda Pitts—Bradsby introduced three changes in company marketing.

First, he realized the limitations of brand-name marketing in which the company, in effect, competed against itself by selling bats such as the "Buster Brown" model that would undercut the better, but more expensive, Louisville Slugger models. So he instituted a "push rule" that required wholesale

*Crack of the Bat: The Louisville Slugger Story*

customers to buy one Louisville Slugger bat for a certain number of brand-name bats, with the ratios to vary.

In 1914, the company launched a focused campaign to sell to the growing youth market by offering "Louisville Sluggers Juniors." The bats were shaped like the bats of the famous players, and had their autographs on them, but were small enough for kids to swing.

In 1919, Hillerich & Bradsby launched an aggressive, focused advertising and promotional campaign to overcome what was still a name-recognition problem. The company had depended on traveling salesmen and trade advertising to sell its Louisville Slugger bats. That advertising would reach the jobbers and retailers, but did not reach the ultimate consumer: the millions of kids playing baseball.

The *Sports Marketing Quarterly* article said the baseball bat business had become very competitive by 1919. Bat companies had begun merging, or acquiring other, smaller firms (e.g., Hillerich & Bradsby bought the Granberg Company). Of the 28 companies remaining in 1919, 20 used strong national advertising.

**Slugging his way toward the World's Series**

**CUYLER**

*of Murderers' Row*

As a boy, Cuyler liked fishing and swimming better than baseball, but made a good record on his high school team.

With Chevrolet he led the semi-pro Industrial League in batting and signed with Bay City of the Michigan-Ontario League, who sold him to the Pittsburgh Pirates.

While farmed out to Charleston, he led the South Carolina League in stolen bases.

While farmed to Nashville, he was voted the most valuable player in the Southern League.

After five years with the Pirates, he was sold to Chicago, where he has won immortality as a member of the Cub's famous murderers' row.

This year he is batting .366.

Like his "partners in crime", Hornsby, Wilson, Grimm and Stephenson, he uses the Louisville Slugger Bat.

Hillerich & Bradsby Co., *Incorporated*, Mfrs., Louisville, Kentucky.

LOUISVILLE SLUGGER
HILLERICH&BRADSBY Cº
LOUISVILLE, KY.
TRADE MARK REG. U.S. PAT. OFF.

ALL LOUISVILLE SLUGGER BATS ARE NOW MADE WITH BONE-RUBBED FINISH AT NO EXTRA COST

What's in a Name?
*Name recognition was important when it came to selling bats, and few names were more distinctive than Kiki Cuyler's of the Pittsburgh Pirates, Chicago Cubs and Brooklyn Dodgers.*

**Famous Slugger.** *Famous Slugger ads (top) featuring Babe Ruth and Lou Gehrig sold a lot of bats.*

**Ask the Bat Boy.** *Louisville Slugger ads (bottom) featuring real bat boys were a great lure for the younger generation.*

In the spring of 1919, Hillerich & Bradsby aggressively swung into national advertising with a four-part sales program. Its ads appeared in magazines such as *Athletic Journal, Popular Mechanic, The American Boy, Boy's Life, The Sporting News* and *Youth's Companion*, which had a combined readership of more than one million.

It began distributing its *Famous Slugger* pamphlets, which over the next 60 years became a sports icon almost as famous as the bats. The pamphlets were distributed by the millions to jobbers and retailers, who were encouraged to pass them on to their customers.

The pamphlets included pictures of famous players, batting tips, season and career records, and inspirational messages for young major league hopefuls. The pamphlets quickly became collectors' items, with boys saving them from season to season.

Hillerich & Bradsby continued advertising in trade magazines, but used those ads to promote the Famous Slugger pamphlets and to tell retailers of their national advertising campaign. The fourth part of the campaign was the slogan "Ask the bat boy—he knows." It ran with pictures of real major league bat boys at work in the dugout. Its message was powerful, emotional; aspiring ballplayers could identify with the batboys, the heroes around them and their bats.

The "push rule" achieved early success, but an economic turndown and general marketing difficulties cut into sales. Hillerich & Bradsby sold about 216,000 bats in 1913, but only about 12,000 of them were the better "Louisville Slugger" bats.

World War I cut deeply into bat sales, but soon after the war, the national advertising and promotion campaign—which changed little from 1919 to 1923—had a dramatic effect. According to the *Sports Marketing Quarterly*, total bat sales increased from 276,000 in 1919 to approximately 1,680,000 in 1923. Louisville Slugger sales during that span increased from approximately 144,000 to 600,000.

More important, autograph-model sales increased from 72,000 in 1919 to approximately 480,000 in 1923. The top four moneymakers for Hillerich & Bradsby in 1923 were the Babe Ruth autograph model, the Ty Cobb autograph model, the Slugger Special, and the George Sisler autograph model. By 1923, Hillerich & Bradsby had become the recognized leader in bat manufacturing.

This was a golden era in sports, and the company had many other ideas for keeping its name before the public. It had created colorful decals to go on its bats—bright, multicolored images of the game's greatest names. It produced posters and advertising that retailers could hang on their walls.

The company heavily promoted the game's greatest legends, such as Rogers Hornsby and Babe Ruth.

Hornsby—properly nicknamed "The Rajah"—was a lifetime .358 hitter over 2,259 games with four clubs. He was tough, motivated, opinionated and, at times, belligerent, running team owners out of the clubhouse if he didn't want to be bothered. But the fans loved him for what he did on the field.

**Home Run Race.**
*Long before the 1990s Sosa-McGwire home run duel, Babe Ruth and Lou Gehrig were doing the same in 1927.*

With all due apologies to Michael Jordan, no one ever had a greater impact on any sport than Ruth. He was the gilded edge of the golden era, the Absolute King of the only professional sport that mattered: baseball.

When Babe Ruth and Lou Gehrig held the country enthralled in 1927 with their incredible home run race—much as Mark McGwire and Sammy Sosa would do 70 years later—Hillerich & Bradsby supplied its dealers with posters that contained places where fans could mark the home runs and play along. When Ruth died in 1948, the company sent out posters of "The Babe" in memoriam.

Hillerich & Bradsby also continued its long tradition of having its sales staff—and company executives—visit spring training and minor and major league ballparks to stay in touch personally. They included Henry Morrow, who began sweeping sawdust from the factory floors in 1901 and would go on to be Hillerich & Bradsby's professional baseball representative for more than 30 years.

Morrow went to spring training every year to talk with the players. He would follow up by attending at least 50 games and the World Series, always eager to discuss bats and baseball. Along the way, he continually searched for new talent to sign up for Louisville Slugger bats.

# PAGES FOR THE AGES

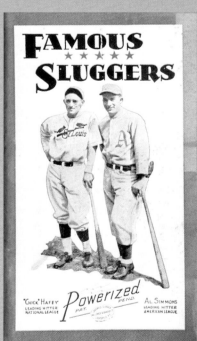

for more than 50 years, the Famous Slugger yearbooks were as eagerly anticipated by baseball fans—especially kids—as opening day itself. Part of that was genetic; baseball fans have a deep-seated need to devour statistics, and the yearbooks were stuffed with batting averages and hitting records.

Another reason was the photographs of the game's stars. When the Famous Slugger yearbooks were introduced in the 1920s, there was no television, no *Sports Illustrated*, no swimsuit edition to get winter-weary fans to April's opening day.

The 1926 edition of the yearbook—actually named Famous Sluggers of 1926—had grainy photographs of the greats from Lou "Buster" Gehrig to the long-forgotten Heinie Manush, the 1926 American League batting champion; he hit .378 to Babe Ruth's mere .372.

The Famous Slugger yearbooks were distributed from the 1920s to the 1970s in retail stores, among wholesale dealers and as promotions in *The Sporting News*.

Over those years, Famous Slugger yearbooks also offered the kind of anecdotes baseball fans need for dessert. The 1940 yearbook told us that "Abraham Lincoln was the first baseball-minded President. He was taking part in a baseball game when notified of his nomination. It was reported that he remarked, 'They'll have to wait a few minutes until I make another base hit.' Luckily for all of us, his quotability improved a great deal by the time he got to the Gettysburg Address.

Another Famous Slugger yearbook of that era pointed out that, after the 1930 season, baseball owners had begun to fret that the ball was too lively; all those home runs were ruining their game. The owners adopted a softer ball in 1931, and total home runs dropped from 1,565 in 1930 to 1,068 in 1931, somewhat mirroring the Great Depression.

Speaking of statistics, the Famous Slugger yearbooks also put the modern home run in a little clearer perspective by pointing out how monumentally deep the center-field fences were in the 1930s and 1940s, before modern parks were built and the fences moved in.

In the American League, it was 450 feet in Chicago, 455 feet in Detroit, 467 feet in Cleveland and an incredible 490 feet in New York, although the right-field line in Yankee Stadium was less than 300 feet, requiring not much of a Ruthian shot.

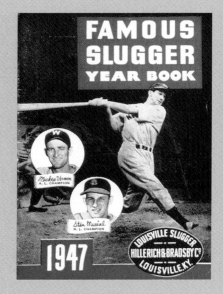

In the National League, the center-field fences included 450 feet in St. Louis, 457 feet in Pittsburgh, 466 feet in Brooklyn and a monstrous 505 feet in New York, where the right-field line was a puny 257 feet, 8 inches.

The Famous Slugger yearbook also appealed directly to kids by showing a series of ads that were titled "Ask the bat boy—he knows." The ads featured batboys apparently giving hitting advice to Babe Ruth and Lou Gehrig, or at least convincing them of the magic in the Louisville Slugger.

They featured advertisements of bats, including the "Kork Grip" bat, patented with an oil-tempered finish, which sold for $2.50 in 1926. Or kids could buy the "Junior Slugger" model, with its burnished finish and golden handle, for a more reasonable 75 cents—still a couple of days' pay in 1926. Smaller kids' bats of that era were even more affordable, "Hillerich's CrackerJack" bat sold for 25 cents, the Junior League youth's bat for 35 cents.

By 1978, the Famous Slugger yearbook was advertising—without a price listing—the PowerBalance aluminum bat, which was perfectly swing weighted—almost like a golf club—for the light, medium and heavy hitters.

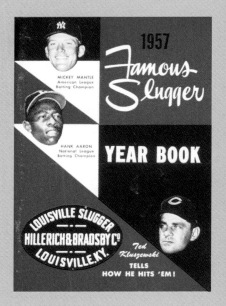

Caring for bats—especially wooden bats—was a recurring article of faith in the Famous Slugger yearbooks. From the 1940s through the 1960s, bat owners were cautioned to winterize their wooden bats by rubbing them with linseed oil and a liquid wax. It was also suggested they rub a bone against the bat to close its pores and protect it—unless you could train your dog to do it.

But mostly, the Famous Slugger yearbook was popular for its hitting and fielding tips. The 1926 version is memorable for flowery language used in explaining its purpose:

> THE DISCERNING WILL GLEAN FROM PERUSAL OF THESE PAGES TWO SIGNIFICANT FACTS:
> FIRST: IT'S THE BAT THAT MAKES BASEBALL, THE CRASH OF ASH ON HORSE HIDE THAT LIFTS THE STANDS TO THEIR FEET, HITTING—SINGLES, DOUBLE, TRIPLES, HOMERUNS—THAT GIVES THE BIG PUNCH TO THE GREAT NATIONAL GAME.
> SECOND: ONE MAKER OF BAT STANDS SUPREME IN BASEBALL'S HALF-CENTURY—AND THAT BAT CARRIES AN OVAL TRADEMARK INCLOSING THE WORDS, *LOUISVILLE SLUGGER*.

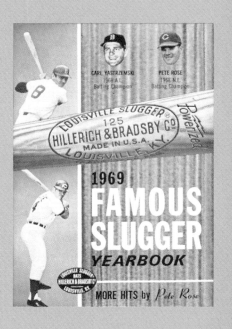

Somewhat toned down in rhetoric, the 1966 yearbook offered some basic hitting tips by Harry "The Hat" Walker. In 1973, Dick Allen, who swung a 42-inch bat, explained the hitting techniques that led him to become a much-feared hitter while also managing to lead the league in strikeouts.

But defense also has its place in the Famous Slugger yearbooks; one year, Pee Wee Reese offered an entire book on how to field.

**Old-Fashioned Service.**
*Henry Morrow personalized bat service as a player representative for 30 years.*

By today's multimillion-dollar standards, the players signed for very little money. One display in the new Louisville Slugger Museum is the endorsement contract Babe Ruth signed for $100 in 1918—the year he led the American League in home runs with 11. Years later, Joe DiMaggio, then 19 years old, signed a contract for $25, with another $25 if he broke any records. That was in 1933, during the Depression, three years before he joined the New York Yankees. Ted Williams would sign for $200 in the 1930s.

Even those figures seem high when compared to a 20-year Hillerich & Bradsby contract signed by infielder/outfielder Ben Chapman on April 24, 1929. Chapman signed for—as the contract stated—"One Dollar."

The endorsements didn't mean the players had to use the bats; the agreement only allowed that their names be used for advertising. Hillerich & Bradsby didn't feel compelled to offer much more; it had no guarantees, either. For every 50 players signed in the minor leagues, perhaps one would make it to the major leagues, and few of those would project enough star quality to sell many bats.

Once they became firmly established, modern major league stars could make some money with their names—and their bats. Various contract incentives provided Roberto Clemente with $3,000 when he collected his 3,000th hit. Henry Aaron was paid $7,000 for the bat with which he hit home runs Nos. 699 and 700—a bat now on display in the Louisville Slugger Museum.

There also were many occasions when the old-line baseball players, often uneducated, unsophisticated or just plain unscrupulous, were more than willing to sign contracts with more than one company. Competing bat companies had to keep lists of their signees, comparing them regularly. One list included a player—Curtis Walker—who signed with Hillerich & Bradsby and Spalding four days apart. His batting eye was a little better; Walker had a 12-year career, batting a lifetime .304 with three teams—but his name belonged to Spalding.

There were also no guarantees on the product. Although a few firms did guarantee bats in their early years, it was not a wise practice; bats—like records—were made to be broken. Hillerich & Bradsby would receive many letters about broken bats—especially as the players demanded lighter bats and skinnier handles—but the company had a memorandum on the subject that it sent to all its dealers:

> The Hillerich & Bradsby Company's policy on guaranteeing bats is unchanged. We do not guarantee bats against breaking, no matter how they are held, and we believe that any policy that encourages unlimited demands for replacement only means grief for dealer, jobber and manufacturer. Bats of wood cannot be made immune from breaking. When a bat is returned to us that is clearly defective, we welcome the opportunity to make replacement. That has always been our policy. But most bats are broken through accident or misuse and no one can be held responsible for conditions beyond his control.

Finzer Factory.
*When Hillerich & Bradsby began selling golf clubs, it moved into this factory complex on Finzer Street in Louisville.*

# ERNIE BANKS

KINGS OF SWING WHO MADE THE SLUGGERS SING

KINGS OF SWING WHO MADE THE SLUGGERS SING

KINGS OF SWING WHO MADE THE SLUGGERS SING

KINGS OF SWING WHO MADE THE SLUGGERS SING

KINGS OF SWING WHO MADE THE SLUGGERS SING

As graceful off the field as he was on it, Ernie Banks had a connection to baseball history even before he stepped on a major league diamond: He was signed for the Negro American League's Kansas City Monarchs by the legendary James T. "Cool Papa" Bell.

In 1953, Banks became the first black player for the Chicago Cubs—six long years after the Dodgers brought up Jackie Robinson. Banks won the National League's Most Valuable Player awards in 1958 and 1959 on teams that personified the Cubs' long tradition of lovable mediocrity. From 1955 to 1960, he hit more home runs—248—than anyone else in major league baseball, including Mickey Mantle, Willie Mays and Hank Aaron.

Banks had grown up in Dallas and was a high school star in football, basketball and track. Though he cared more about softball than baseball, he joined a black barnstorming team at 17—for $15 a game. At age 21—and after two years in the Army—he was playing shortstop on the north side of Chicago.

Like Aaron, Banks hit with his wrists, waiting on pitches, practically stealing the ball from the catcher's mitt before driving it into the outfield. Banks always liked the way a good bat felt in his hands.

"It was Hillerich & Bradsby, the Louisville Slugger, who really contributed to a lot of our success in baseball," Banks said at the 1996 opening of the Louisville Slugger Museum. "To be able to have that kind of bat, sometimes our own specific models, that feel good in our hands, to see how the bats are made, to see the people who work here, the love they put into the product is something I enjoyed."

Jack McGrath, a vice president for advertising and marketing, said, "The craze proved a godsend to Hillerich & Bradsby. It was just getting into full swing when the stock market crashed in 1929.

"Our golf plant was working 13 hours each day, Monday through Friday, and from 7 a.m. to 4 p.m. on Saturdays. There was also a night shift, which started at 9 o'clock each night, the moment the day shift workers started for home. We were making putters, putters, putters!

"But there did come a day when not a single golf order was received and then our golf factory became a very quiet place for the next two or three years."

**Ward and Babe.**
*Personal service included Ward Hillerich taking Babe Ruth to the 1934 Kentucky Derby.*

In the 1930s, the company was also producing softball bats for a growing market—at home and abroad. The baseball bat business continued to grow, but much less vigorously. Great players of the day continued to visit the factory and were entertained at the Kentucky Derby. Entire teams would occasionally visit the factory, traveling north from spring training.

Bud Hillerich was his company's greatest figurehead. He rarely missed a World Series; he would send his friends—and favorite players—National and American League World Series bats autographed by the players. In 1923 and again in 1935, Hillerich went on a world baseball tour, the latter including a tour of Japan with Babe Ruth and Lou Gehrig.

Occasional disasters continued to plague the company. In June 1931, a fire swept through one of its lumber storage yards at Preston Street and Burnett Avenue, destroying about $500,000 worth of would-be baseball bats and golf clubs.

**Up in Smoke, Again.**
*A 1931 fire destroyed two million pieces of ash and hickory used to make bats and golf clubs.*

Rainout.
*The 1937 flood buried Louisville—and Hillerich & Bradsby—under six feet of water.*

*FLOOD EDITION No. 2*

# The Courier-Journal and TIMES

Published January 26, 1937, In the Offices of The Shelby News and The Shelby Sentinel, Shelbyville, Ky.

## Martial Law Is Declared In Louisville

**Crest of Flood For Louisville Set At 58 Feet**

Waters' Rise Too Fast For Engineers to Keep Maps.

**Phone Service Crumbling, Two Exchanges Are Cut Off**

Scarlet Fever, Measles Break Out Among Refugees and Typhoid Is Called Inevitable; Gasoline Issued For Relief Only; Milk Supply Good.

**Refugees Are Rushed From City By Train**

Residents of Downtown Area Taken to Crescent Hill, La Grange.

**Louisville Police Ordered To Shoot Down All Looters**

Director of Safety Announces Food, Clothing, Gasoline, Other Articles to Be Confiscated; Profiteering Is Fought.

**5 Companies Of U.S. Troops Move On City**

600 Are to Assist Mayor In Flood Rescue Fight.

---

The fire started in a garage near the two-acre yard and burned furiously for about five hours, consuming about two million pieces of ash and hickory that had been seasoning for about two years. Not one piece of wood was saved, but a company spokesman said there was enough lumber at two other yards to keep golf club and bat production going.

Then, in the bitter winter of 1937, the entire Hillerich & Bradsby bat and golf club complex was partially submerged, buried beneath the worst flood in Ohio River history.

The Ohio Valley had been battered with rain for weeks, the ground too frozen to allow the water to soak in. The water then gushed into the ancient Hillerich & Bradsby complex on January 23 by forcing its way into the drains. Within days, there was water six feet deep in many Louisville streets, occupying almost two-thirds of the town.

Jack McGrath, who rowed back and forth to his office in a boat, wrote, "For days we were paralyzed, and even following the flood things were a sorry mess. For example our front office at Jackson and Finzer was full of ice, mud and broken windows, and debris was everywhere. The clean-up job was just one of the nastiest projects that we ever had to do."

But McGrath did find a little humor in the situation: "The first thing done was to remove to the second floor the private liquor stock (private, pre-Prohibition stuff, naturally) of Mr. Bradsby, and some belonging to the company, that had for years been stored in the basement vault.

"Then, all machinery such as polishing and grinding lathes, the drilling machines, etc., were covered with a heavy coating of grease. In those days we

*Crack of the Bat: The Louisville Slugger Story*

still had a lot of belt-driven machinery and one of the biggest jobs done by the emergency crew was to take down the overhead motors secured to the ceiling."

The skeleton crew stayed in the golf factory, sleeping on burlap and eating sandwiches. There was no electricity or water—at least not drinkable water. Frank Bradsby and Stanley Held flew to Cleveland to buy pumps—a commodity sought by every flooded factory in the Ohio River Valley. A temporary office was established in the home of Bud Hillerich, and cleanup began. On February 3, bat shipments resumed from old stock, which had been safe on the second floor. Other railroad cars filled with bats followed, some from stock sent to higher ground in the first days of the flood. It would be February 22—a month after the flood struck—before normal bat production resumed.

In a story in the February 1937 *Sporting Good Dealer*—written again to assure the athletic equipment world that Hillerich & Bradsby could survive fire and flood—Frank Bradsby said, "Every man in our organization knew what his work was, knew how to do it, and took hold with a will. We accomplished a month's work in the first week of our re-occupation."

The flood, unfortunately, would take its greatest toll on the stressed, hard-working Bradsby, who died in May 1937 at age 59. He suffered a heart

**Harridge and Bradsby.**
*American League president William Harridge (left) and Frank Bradsby (right) are shown touring the bat factory in 1934.*

By 1939, Hillerich &
Bradsby was shipping
millions of bats around the
country.

attack on a train while returning from Washington, D.C. He had been in the capital, lobbying for an end to a federal excise tax on sporting goods.

He had been a giant in the sporting goods field, having been elected president of the Athletic Goods Manufacturers Association 16 consecutive terms, and six times was president of the National Association of Golf Club Manufacturers.

So valued was Bradsby in the field that he was among the five legendary figures first elected to the sporting goods Hall of Fame. The other four were John Browning, who patented the Winchester single-shot rifle; Ole Evinrude, who launched the outboard motor industry; James Heddon, who developed early fishing lures; and A.G. Spalding, founder of the famous sporting goods company.

Bradsby had no immediate survivors. His share of the company was placed in trust in St. Louis banks until the Hillerich family bought out his nieces and nephews in 1968. At his death, longtime assistant John T. Rodgers was named secretary-treasurer and sales manager.

As the United States rose from the Depression, so did the bat business. A 1940 story in the *Sunday New York Herald-Tribune* said that from a "dingy, sprawling red brick building in the manufacturing section of this horse-racing city" the company was turning out 2,000,000 bats a year—with about 40,000 of them used by professional players.

"All those bats are still sold directly to players in organized ball without the intervention of a middleman, and a model of every bat ever made for a big league player is on file in the archives."

At the time, the company employed about 350 men and women, with almost five million billets of wood being seasoned at a 10-acre yard nearby. Each year about two million billets were sent to the company, the wood replaced by "green ash" sent in from the woods. About 90 percent of professional baseball was swinging Louisville Sluggers.

Then Hillerich & Bradsby—like most companies in the United States—again had to change gears, this time to make gun stocks and tank Caterpillar track "pins" for the U.S. military in World War II. Once again, Jack McGrath had written a brief history of that period.

"We were making fine progress in the years just prior to World War II," he wrote. "Except for Hanna we had no competition in the bat business, and we were making fine progress with our golf lines, too. After our entry in the war we pushed as hard as ever, knowing full well, as everyone else did, the wartime restrictions were in store for us."

The war ended golf club production, but a "centerless grinder" in that department was used to turn out thousands of Caterpillar track pins. Using bat factory equipment, the company also produced more than one million M-1 carbine gun stocks. It also produced rolling pins, potato mashers and thousands of hitting cudgels of another kind—police billy clubs.

"Used by air wardens, police departments, ordnance works, Navy yards, Army yards, air bases, defense plants and ship yards," the advertising

**Gun Mettle.**
*During World War II, with most men in the service, women were sanding the M-1 carbine gun stocks made by Hillerich & Bradsby.*

**War Club.**
*The company turned out millions of police billy clubs during the war.*

**Battling Back.**
*With baseball and golf now in the background, the company advertised its war effort.*

said. "Turned from high grade hickory wood, lacquered finish, overall length 23 inches, rawhide thong. List price—$1 each."

The company continued to turn out baseball and softball bats, but almost all of them were shipped to the armed forces around the world, with only a few—outside of the professional bats—getting into civilian hands.

"Just because you were operating a war production plant, you still had to go out and get men and materials," McGrath wrote. "And much of what you were looking for was desperately hard to find. As might be guessed, men were especially difficult to come by."

As a result, many of the production jobs were handled by women, especially in making the M-1 carbine stocks. Raw material for bats was especially hard to find. Many of the firm's salespeople had to be let go, or else they were doubled up on other jobs. In 1944, about 200 people worked at the firm, but more than 40 of them had been with the company 19 years or longer.

"That eternal problem—timber procurement—was never worse," McGrath said. "Despite the fact that a very high percentage of our production was going to the Army and the Navy, we still had to go out in the woods and on the farms and find people who would get timber out for us."

Near the end of the war, Hillerich & Bradsby was honored by Army-Navy officials with an "E" award for military effort.

"Cool Papa" Bell.
*James Thomas "Cool Papa" Bell swung a Louisville Slugger in the Negro leagues, was voted into the Baseball Hall of Fame in 1974.*

The war had greatly diminished the professional baseball talent pool and created a new sports phenomenon, the All-American Girls Professional Baseball League, which also used Louisville Slugger bats. Created by Phil Wrigley, owner of the Chicago Cubs, the short-lived league had teams such as the Grand Rapids Chicks, Battle Creek Belles, Kalamazoo Lassies and the Rockford Peaches—whose story was recounted in the movie "A League of Their Own."

Hillerich & Bradsby also supplied the Negro leagues with bats during the 1920s, '30s and '40s. Historian Jack McGrath had on file letters of appreciation from William "Judy" Johnson, who batted .301 for 17 years, and James Thomas "Cool Papa" Bell, who played baseball 29 years and batted .337 in a 20-year professional career. He was named to the Hall of Fame in 1974.

# ROBIN YOUNT

*KINGS OF SWING WHO MADE THE SLUGGERS SING*

*KINGS OF SWING WHO MADE THE SLUGGERS SING*

*KINGS OF SWING WHO MADE THE SLUGGERS SING*

*KINGS OF SWING WHO MADE THE SLUGGERS SING*

*KINGS OF SWING WHO MADE THE SLUGGERS SING*

Robin Yount's most magical baseball year came in 1982, when he led the Milwaukee Brewers into the World Series with a .331 batting average, 210 hits and a league-leading .578 slugging percentage. He was named Most Valuable Player and won a Gold Glove at shortstop.

He was 27 years old, but already in his ninth year of major league baseball. He had been only 18—one of the youngest starters in big-league history—when he broke in with the Brewers in 1974, batting .250 in 107 games.

In 1986, he was the seventh-youngest player in major league history to collect 2,000 hits. He picked up another 1,142 hits during the next seven years—enough to propel him into the Hall of Fame in 1998 with George Brett and Nolan Ryan in the first year all three men were eligible.

Yount—to the best of his recollection—did almost all of it holding a Louisville Slugger.

"There might have been a few times, I know if there was I could count them on one hand, when I might have tried something else," he said at the 1996 Louisville Slugger Museum opening.

"An athlete, you know, is always looking for an edge somewhere, but I know for sure I always ended up with a Louisville Slugger back in my hands. It never lasted more than a bat or two with something other than a Louisville Slugger."

**Milwaukee MVP.**
*Robin Yount heads toward first base.*

**Reese and Robinson.**
*Pee Wee Reese and Jackie Robinson joined together to lead the Brooklyn Dodgers to an elusive World Series championship in 1955.*

At the end of World War II, big-league baseball came roaring back, eager, like everyone in the country, to get on with life. Its stars—many whose careers had been interrupted by the war—included Ted Williams, Stan Musial, Ralph Kiner, Joe DiMaggio, Pee Wee Reese and Jackie Robinson.

Reese was born in the small town of Ekron, Kentucky. He had grown up in Louisville and played for the AAA Louisville Colonels in 1938 (for $150 a month) before joining the Brooklyn Dodgers in 1940. Always loyal to Louisville and the Louisville Slugger, the Hall of Famer would represent Hillerich & Bradsby for years after his retirement from baseball, working with Rex Bradley, manager of professional and college baseball sales.

Robinson, the first black man allowed to play major league baseball in the 20th century, joined Brooklyn in 1947. It was an earth-shattering time for baseball—and the country—where black men had gone off to fight and die for a freedom that few were permitted to enjoy once they returned home.

Robinson, a hero and savior to black America, was cursed and booed by many white fans and opposing players. Three of his Brooklyn teammates drew up a petition saying they would rather be traded than play with him.

Reese has always been credited with helping ease that transition, the most famous instance occurring in the game in which he went over and put an arm around Robinson's shoulder when fans began jeering him. Reese, who became the Dodgers' captain, obviously refused to sign the petition.

*Crack of the Bat: The Louisville Slugger Story*

Pee Wee Reese.
*Brooklyn Dodger Pee Wee Reese hurdled many obstacles on his way to the Hall of Fame.*

**Third Generation.**
*John A. "Junie" Hillerich ran the company from 1950 to 1969.*

"If he can take my job," Reese told a reporter, "he's entitled to it."

Robinson, who died in 1972, and Reese, who died in 1999, would both be honored on the 50th anniversary of Robinson's breaking the racial barrier, in ceremonies at the Louisville Slugger Museum.

The 1940s also brought many changes in the Hillerich & Bradsby family. John T. Rodgers died in 1945. J.A. "Bud" Hillerich, the company president and baseball legend, died of a heart attack in Chicago's Palmer House on Nov. 28, 1946. He was on a trip to professional baseball meetings in Los Angeles. He was being treated for heart trouble and had been urged to stay home. He was 80 years old.

*Crack of the Bat: The Louisville Slugger Story*

Bud was succeeded by his oldest son, Ward A. Hillerich, who died on Nov. 27, 1949, after a long illness. In 1950, Ward was succeeded by his brother, J.A. "Junie" Hillerich Jr., who would head the company until his death in 1969.

Junie Hillerich faced a challenge unseen by the other men who headed the company: labor unions and labor strife. After World War II, many Hillerich & Bradsby employees voted to join the United Steel Workers of America Local 3931. Labor negotiations were often contentious, with strikes closing the company in 1950, and several other times in the 1960s and 1970s, including a six-week strike by about 400 workers in 1969.

Led by Junie Hillerich, the company grew and diversified extensively in the 1950s and '60s. The firm acquired extensive holdings in timber mills, mostly in Pennsylvania and New York. Golf had become a "television sport," and PowerBilt sales were booming, especially in Japan and other Asian countries. Plans were made to push bat sales in Mexico, Canada, Latin America and into Japan, where baseball would become a passion, thanks in part to the Babe Ruth and Bud Hillerich tours of that country.

The PowerBilt reputation grew with the success of touring professionals who used the clubs, including Bobby Nichols, winner of the 1964 Professional Golf Association championship; Gay Brewer, 1967 Masters winner; Frank Beard, leading money winner in 1969; and Charles Coody, 1971 Masters winner. More recently, Fuzzy Zoeller, the 1979 Masters winner, and Isao Aoki and Miller Barber have had success using the clubs.

The company also opened its factory to tours, hosting a wide variety of groups from Little Leaguers to professional teams to groups of tourists—

**Bobby Nichols.**
*Bobby Nichols championed PowerBilt golf clubs.*

**Seeing How It's Done.**
*Factory tours have long been a part of the company's sales efforts.*

both men and women—who wanted to see, hear and smell white ash being transformed into baseball bats.

The company inaugurated the "Silver Bat" award given annually to National and American League batting champions, with Jackie Robinson winning the National League award in 1949 and George Kell the American League award. Later came the "Silver Slugger" awards honoring the best offensive players at each position.

Tony Gwynn has won eight Silver Bats, more than any other player in history, including four in a row from 1994 to 1997. Rod Carew has won seven bats, Wade Bogs five and Stan Musial, Roberto Clemente and Bill Madlock four each.

In 1980, Hillerich & Bradsby inaugurated the Silver Slugger awards, featuring the best offensive players at each position, as picked by the managers and coaches from each league.

Hillerich & Bradsby had also begun sponsorship of the very popular World Series films, which showed highlights of the previous year's Series to organizations all over the United States. In addition, a traveling "Famous Bat" show featured bats used by players over the years.

Bat sales grew steadily. Officials said in 1956 the company was making nearly 3 million baseball and softball bats, more than its two top competitors, McLaughlin-Millard at Dodgeville, N.Y., and the Hanna Manufacturing Co. of Athens, Georgia, combined. In 1959 the company celebrated making its one hundred millionth bat.

by 1967, Hillerich & Bradsby was making between four and five million bats a year—and the company still dominated the professional market. Business, in fact, was too good for the company's antiquated facilities, with golf production spread across several floors of a nearly 100-year-old building, and its bat factory aisles so choked with material, there was barely room to get a dolly through. Constantly, employees had to load and unload dollies, pushing them from place to place, to get the bats made. Parking outside the building, in an industrial area, was at a premium, and occasionally dangerous.

In the late 1960s—with golf booming and bat sales approaching $7 million a year—company officials began looking for a new home. The search was made that much more difficult by the death of Junie Hillerich, who died on Jan. 5, 1969, in his winter home near Sarasota, Florida, after a long illness. He was 57. In May 1969, John A. "Jack" Hillerich III, at 29, was named company president.

Jack Hillerich, a Vanderbilt University graduate with a degree in economics, had been with the firm during college, and joined it permanently in 1961. In his early years with the company, he had spent two years working in bat timber yards in New York and Pennsylvania. His other duties included a year and a half as an assistant to Frank J. Ryan, then the sales manager for professional baseball bats. Hillerich and his immediate family now hold controlling interest in the privately held firm, with some stock owned by employees and descendants of former employees.

**Mathews and Aaron.**
*Milwaukee Braves Eddie Mathews
and Hank Aaron, the latter
displaying his Silver Bat award.*

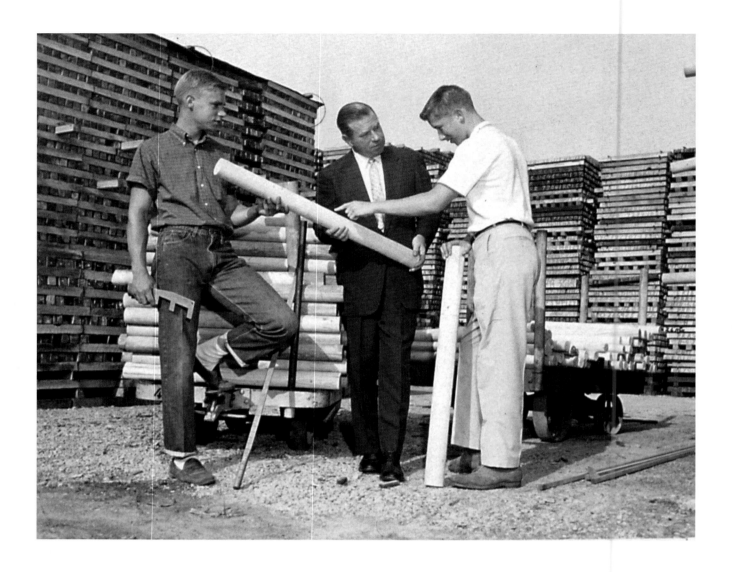

**Out in the Yard.**
*In this 1958 photo, company president John A. Hillerich Jr. (center) shows a wooden billet to sons Jack III (left) and Hart.*

"I was involved on October 27, 1940," said Hillerich, who represented the fourth generation of his family to lead the company. "That was the day I was born."

Hillerich leaned heavily on the expertise of a veteran employee, Bill Becker. Hillerich's first task was to find a new home for his company—where rumors had been circulating for years that it had to go "somewhere." He said his primary responsibility was to his 600 employees; he did not want to leave Kentucky, or Louisville. He considered plans to rebuild or move into an existing facility.

"I had a very good group of loyal people and I did not want to lose any of them," he said.

Hillerich had promised his employees they would be the first to know of any move, a promise that eventually required such secrecy that only a few top officials—and not all of their wives—knew the final decision. It became public in October 1972, when Hillerich chartered Greyhound buses and led his employees to their new home—near Clarksville, Indiana. Not even the bus driver was aware of the final destination.

*Crack of the Bat: The Louisville Slugger Story*

Hillerich—able to laugh about it later—remembers the reaction of publicist Jack McGrath as the bus left Louisville and headed across the Ohio River into Indiana.

"So we're in the middle of the bridge," Hillerich said, "and he said, 'Oh, my God, do you know what you've done?'"

Taking the Louisville Slugger to Indiana was traumatic—with jokes about the "Jeffersonville Slugger" sure to follow. But waiting just a few miles across the river was a modern, empty, air-conditioned, one-story, 114,000-square-foot building that once housed a piano factory—and was built for woodworking.

"So here was this opportunity four miles away," Hillerich said. "A new building and all these wonderful engineering devices that I knew would improve our quality.

"In the old place we were processing seven million pieces of timber a year and we did not own a forklift. We didn't have room."

Surrounding the expansive new building were 60 acres of land, a nearby rail spur and Interstate 65. During the next two years, the company would move all its golf and bat-making capabilities to Indiana, but keep its

**Jeffersonville Slugger.**
*In 1972, the Louisville Slugger left Louisville for a new home in southern Indiana, bringing worried cries of the "Indiana Slugger."*

**Slugger Park.**
*An aerial view of Slugger Park in southern Indiana.*

company headquarters and mailing address in Louisville. It would expand the building to about 260,000 square feet and add a side yard for bat storage.

"We made a lot of money over there," said Hillerich. "It was a very good business decision . . . and I don't think I'd do it again."

The move would include a $4.5 million expansion. In the new home, golf-club business expanded and bat production hit almost seven million. But waiting on the horizon was the greatest change that baseball—and Hillerich & Bradsby—would ever face: the aluminum bat. It would provide the company with both a challenge and a tremendous opportunity.

The change had been coming for years. Giving baseball players the thinner, lighter bats they wanted made the wooden bats more vulnerable to breakage. At the same time, improving technology made better aluminum bats available as youth leagues, softball leagues, high schools and colleges began looking for ways to cut costs.

Aluminum bats may have changed the "crack" of the bat to the "bonk" of modern baseball, but they were durable, and softballs and baseballs would jump off them faster and farther. When the National Collegiate Athletic Association legalized aluminum bats in 1974, the door swung wide open.

The saving grace for baseball purists was that professional baseball, fearing injury from bigger, stronger players using trampoline-like aluminum bats, did not legalize them.

*Crack of the Bat: The Louisville Slugger Story*

Hillerich & Bradsby got off to a slow start in the aluminum bat business; its product was not very competitive, and the company initially refused to put its world-famous trademark and stamp of approval on metal. The company recovered after it bought an aluminum bat company in Ontario, California, but the impact of aluminum on wooden bat-making would be enormous. After making about seven million of them in 1972, Hillerich & Bradsby saw the sale of wooden bats begin to fall drastically, down to about a million in the early 1990s.

Bill Williams, company vice president, explained the situation: "Pee Wee Reese came back from spring training one year and he said he had finally seen a piece of what the future might be like. He said he'd seen that first player that had never used a wooden bat.

"We were so afraid we were going to lose a whole generation of baseball. Kids who graduated from college to become high school coaches were using aluminum bats. We were afraid there was going to be a whole generation growing up without Louisville Sluggers. That was why it was paramount we develop an aluminum bat."

The company began to build better aluminum bats and used its customer loyalty to market them. Its TPS, TPX, SLUGGER and AIRATTACK2 models became strong sellers in the high school, college and softball ranks. It

**Youngsters at Play.** *Louisville Slugger bats have always been a part of the Little League World Series.*

**Lisa Fernandez.**
*Olympic softball player Lisa Fernandez used the company's TPS bat.*

promoted the TPS Model bats used by Olympic softball players Lisa Fernandez and Dot Richardson.

Hillerich & Bradsby still dominates the market in wooden bats for professional players; it sells about 200,000 bats a year to the major and minor leagues. Each major league player receives about 90 to 120 bats a year at $27 to $30 each. Overall, Jack Hillerich said, the company does not make money on its wooden bats, but it will keep making them.

"You don't want to get out of the wood business when wood is who you are," he said. "If you walked into a store and tried to sell an aluminum

**Dot Richardson.**
*Olympian Dot Richardson became a company spokesperson for aluminum bats.*

*Crack of the Bat: The Louisville Slugger Story*

**Cammi Granato.**
*Olympic hockey player Cammi Granato endorsed Louisville Hockey sticks.*

bat without being Louisville Slugger, you're nobody. They wouldn't listen to you."

Hillerich & Bradsby compensates by selling about 1.5 million of the much more profitable aluminum bats a year—bats that can cost hundreds of dollars. It needs to hold on to its heritage of wooden bats, but there is more profit in metal.

Hillerich & Bradsby also moved in a big way into women's hockey, outfitting many college teams and the U.S. Olympic team and signing star Cammi Granato to an endorsement contract to swing a "Louisville Hockey" stick. The Canadian subsidiary, located in Wallaceburg, Ontario, produces about 500,000 "Louisville Hockey" sticks each year in 15 different models. These sticks are made for professional and amateur teams in Canada and the United States, as well as in Europe and Japan. But Hillerich estimated about 80 percent of the company income was in baseball products, with 15 percent in hockey and 5 percent in golf.

In the 1990s, the company's aluminum bats were being made in California, and its hockey equipment was being produced in Wallaceburg, Ontario. Golf sales slowed, and wooden bat sales fell to about 15 percent of their peak figures. It meant Hillerich & Bradsby no longer needed all that space in Indiana. What it needed to do—what it wanted to do—was to come back home again to Louisville.

Kentucky, Jefferson County and Louisville officials helped lure the company back. The original proposal for its new Louisville location included a 270-foot steel bat—the St. Louis Gateway Arch of bats—that was to be erected

**Bats on Fence.**
*Aluminum bats changed the face—and sound—of many softball and baseball games.*

# HARMON
# KILLEBREW

*KINGS OF SWING WHO MADE THE SLUGGERS SING*

*KINGS OF SWING WHO MADE THE SLUGGERS SING*

*KINGS OF SWING WHO MADE THE SLUGGERS SING*

*KINGS OF SWING WHO MADE THE SLUGGERS SING*

*KINGS OF SWING WHO MADE THE SLUGGERS SING*

Hammerin' Harmon Killebrew was Mark McGwire before Mark McGwire was cool. Killebrew was a big, gentle man who was never tossed from a game by an umpire—and he played 2,454 games in a span of 22 major league seasons, all but one with the Minnesota Twins and their forerunners, the Washington Senators.

By the age of 31, he had clubbed 380 home runs—more than Babe Ruth at the same age. Injuries "limited" him to another 193 home runs over the next eight years, but his total of 573 is fifth on the all-time list.

Killebrew was signed at 17 from his hometown of Payette, Idaho, becoming a Washington Senator after a U.S. senator from Idaho gave baseball scouts a tip. It didn't take baseball genius; Killebrew batted .847 in high school, and half his hits were home runs.

In the majors, he played every infield position but second base, moved to left field and ended up as a designated hitter.

According to *The Ballplayers*, he once hit a ball over the roof at Tiger Stadium and parked another home run six rows deep in the upper deck at Metropolitan Stadium, breaking two seats about 530 feet from home plate. The seats were painted orange and never sold again.

Of his 2,086 hits in regular-season play, 817 were for extra bases. He led the American League in home runs from 1962 to 1964, hitting 48, 45 and 49 in succession. In 8,147 times at bat, he never laid down a sacrifice bunt.

"Every home run that I hit in the majors was with a Louisville Slugger," Killebrew said at the Louisville Slugger Museum opening. "There was something, I don't want to say, magical, about the Louisville Slugger name, but since I was a small kid, that's all I ever used."

Hammerin' Harmon.
*Harmon Killebrew was one of baseball's all-time great sluggers.*

Louisville Slugger Museum. *Hillerich & Bradsby returned to its Louisville roots in the 1990s in a museum/factory complex anchored by the world's largest bat.*

at the intersection of downtown highways. The proposed bat included an elevator and observation deck, but not enough cleared land was available to get the project on deck, much less to the plate.

Instead, the company went back to its baseball roots: It would build a $14 million combination golf-club-and-baseball-bat factory, office and museum at Main and Eighth streets in downtown Louisville. The proposed site had a familiar look to it: an old, red-brick, Civil War warehouse.

At first, company officials did not like the site; that section of town was worn and decrepit. It took some convincing; Kentucky and Louisville each

**An Indoor Camden Yards.** *The museum features a lifelike re-creation of Baltimore's famed Camden Yards.*

put up about $600,000 to bring back the Louisville Slugger, and a $5.8 million garage was to be built behind the museum.

Once convinced, company officials traveled the country looking at other museums; they were most impressed by the look and feel of a civil rights museum they visited in Birmingham, Alabama. They decided it was most important that the Louisville Slugger Museum honor the game of baseball—not the company that makes its bats.

Museum designers tossed around words like "challenging" and "creative" and "totally spectacular." The Louisville Slugger Museum would still include the world's biggest bat—a 120-foot, 40-ton, Babe Ruth model that now leans casually against the side of the new complex, setting the tone, dominating the whole street. Thousands of passersby a year stop just to be photographed beside the bat.

Inside the museum is a mammoth glove carved from Kentucky limestone by sculptors Albert Nelson and Kim Hillerich, wife of John Hillerich IV, Jack's son. A carved stone ball is tucked inside the glove's webbing, which is another magnet for baseball fans.

**Three Generations.**
*The future of the company: John A. Hillerich V, John A. Hillerich IV and John A. Hillerich III pose inside the museum on a huge glove carved from Kentucky limestone.*

The museum was an instant hit, drawing about 250,000 tourists a year and serving as a catalyst for growth in downtown Louisville. Its 15,000 square feet of space include an introductory movie, then a walk through a dugout and onto a playing field, where Casey Stengel and Mickey Mantle appear to be in earnest discussion.

Beyond that are displays of players' statistics and the bats they used. There are videotapes and audiotapes of some of the great names and moments in baseball history . . . broadcasters Mel Allen and Red Barber . . . Hank Aaron's 715th home run . . . Bobby Thomson's dramatic 1951 home run . . . "the Giants win the pennant . . . the Giants win the pennant" . . . a bat used by Sammy Sosa in the 1998 home run race with Mark McGwire.

One of the most popular exhibits allows visitors to stand—protected—behind a plate while a major league fastball comes at them at 90 miles an hour. There is a gift shop in the museum, and a wall containing more than 7,000 signatures of players who signed Hillerich & Bradsby contracts—from Babe Ruth to George "Twinkletoes" Selkirk to Ken Griffey Jr. Above, circling the museum so employees can look down, are the open, spacious company offices, with baseball memorabilia on display at every curve of the wall.

One of the offices is occupied by John Hillerich IV, 35, president of the PowerBilt division, whose son is John Hillerich V. John IV's plans for the

*Crack of the Bat: The Louisville Slugger Story*

future include pushing Hillerich & Bradsby further into the computer age, perhaps making it the main source of information for all of baseball, as well as a manufacturer of quality bats and athletic equipment.

"There's always been an undercurrent of what our name means," he said. "So I guess I got into the business Aug. 10, 1963, the day I was born."

Behind the office and museum is the working Hillerich & Bradsby factory, where tourists can watch bats being made for professional ballplayers and even order full-sized bats with their names on them.

Chuck Schupp, the man who now handles professional baseball for Hillerich & Bradsby, said the company signs only about 20 to 30 players a

**Chuck Schupp.**
*Hillerich & Bradsby player representative Chuck Schupp on the job.*

**Big Bat.**
*The world's largest bat was paraded down the street on its way to the museum.*

year now. The fee is usually a few hundred dollars and a set of PowerBilt golf clubs for a 20–year contract. For all the changes in the game—and in society—about 60 to 70 percent of major league hitters still swing a Louisville Slugger.

"We pay all the guys the same, basically," Schupp said. "It is a service contract from our company. It's a long-term commitment to say, hey, if you promise to use Louisville Slugger, or make your best efforts to, we will put you in a priority group for service, quality and delivery."

There's another baseball development in downtown Louisville that brings the Louisville Slugger story all the way around the bases. This year, a new Louisville Slugger Field opened for the AAA Louisville RiverBats—of which Jack Hillerich is a part owner.

Including site acquisition, Slugger Field cost about $37 million, giving Louisville one of the finest minor league ballparks in the country, a comfortable, cozy, new-old place holding 13,500 fans, about 11,800 of them in permanent chair-back seats. Designed by HNTB Architects of Kansas City, and K. Norman Berry and Associates of Louisville, the park features a grassy berm behind the left-center-field fence, a vantage point faintly reminiscent of

*Crack of the Bat: The Louisville Slugger Story*

the city's pioneer baseball days when fans stood within grazing distance of the players.

It has chair-back seats in left field for the fans who like a comfortable baseball experience with a view, a four-tiered picnic area and 18-foot over-look in right-center—with a concession stand. Thirty luxury boxes circle home plate above the lower level, their rent making the park financially feasible.

Louisville native and baseball legend Pee Wee Reese is to be honored with a large bronze statue, perhaps in a park just across the street from Slugger Field. Enhancing the rich baseball tradition of nearby Cincinnati, the RiverBats opened the 2000 season as new AAA affiliate of the Reds, who signed hometown favorite Ken Griffey Jr. to a long-term contract. Louisville, the first minor league franchise to draw one million fans in a season, is back on top.

"We already had a home run," RedBirds general manager, vice president and part owner Dale Owens said of the new affiliation. "That made it a grand slam."

The Hillerich & Bradsby Company put up $2 million in "naming rights" to help make it all happen. Unable to escape the company's own history, the ballpark includes an entryway through the doors of a red-brick train shed built in Louisville just about the time J.F. Hillerich began turning bats in a small woodworking shop just down the street.

**The RiverBats' New Home.**
*Louisville Slugger Field.*

# TED WILLIAMS

*KINGS OF SWING WHO MADE THE SLUGGERS SING*

*KINGS OF SWING WHO MADE THE SLUGGERS SING*

*KINGS OF SWING WHO MADE THE SLUGGERS SING*

*KINGS OF SWING WHO MADE THE SLUGGERS SING*

Always looking for a hitting advantage, Boston Red Sox legend Ted Williams would get a jump on the American League opposition even before his bats left the Hillerich & Bradsby factory. Williams would spend time in the factory climbing through the woodpiles looking for the best material—and then coaxing the workers to be sure he got it.

"There was an old guy named Fritz Bickel who made bats," Williams said. "Here I was, this 18- or 19-year-old-kid, and Fritz could see the enthusiasm I had for hitting, so we would talk about bats.

"Then one day I did something. I gave him a $10 tip, which was a lot of money in those days. Anyway, for the rest of my career if he got a piece of wood just like I liked it, with just the right grain and the knot right in the right spot, he'd save it for me.

"Every once in a while I'd get a little package in the mail, and it would be bats from Fritz. He was an awfully nice man, and I sure enjoyed climbing all through the racks picking out what I wanted."

Williams's often-mentioned goal in life was to be the greatest hitter who ever lived—and he was in the ballpark. His .344 lifetime average is sixth best in history. He was the last man to bat over .400 (.406 in 1941), and his 521 home runs rank 10th all time. All that, despite missing almost six full years due to injuries, and his service as a pilot in World War II and the Korean War.

"A good bat has to feel right in your hands," Williams said. "The next thing is balance, weight, weight, weight.

"At first I didn't know what my bats weighed, but after I got models with my name on it I would send the clubhouse boy to the post office to get it weighed on a scale. Finally, we got a scale in the clubhouse."

Williams said he learned early in his career that bat speed is the most important factor in good hitting; his peers were using bats weighing 36 to 43 ounces, but his bats were lighter than that—34 and 35 ounces.

His fussiness about his bats was part of who he was. He didn't like to have his bats ride in the cargo area of an airplane. He didn't like to see any bats left on grass during games: humidity might soak in. He once complained to Hillerich & Bradsby about the taper on the handle of a new bunch of bats. Hillerich & Bradsby officials checked with calipers and found them five-hundredths of an inch off.

Williams could also tell the difference in the weight of his bats. Bud Hillerich once picked out five bats weighing exactly the same, and a sixth weighing a half an ounce more. Williams picked the heavier bat each time. And he stayed loyal to his Louisville Sluggers.

"I think I can hit with any kind of bat," he said, "but I know I wouldn't have had the success had it not been for the Louisville Slugger bats I used the last 25 years of my career. Absolutely, they were the best for me. I tried others once, but I went back to the Louisville Slugger."

The Splendid Splinter.
*Ted Williams*

# MEN AND THEIR BATS

*A LOVE STORY*

Joe's Kiss.
The slick & classy Joe DiMaggio gives his Louisville Slugger bat a token of appreciation.

t hough rarely discussed in public—or, for that matter, in the dugout—no piece of equipment in sport has ever excited a more personal response from its user than a baseball bat.

Check it out. Fully grown men in the tax brackets of Boston bankers will lovingly oil, rub and caress a baseball bat, even kiss its "sweet spot" in joyous clubhouse celebration if the mood hits.

If you need a little historical perspective to such bat lunacy, let the record show that Hall of Famer Eddie Collins would bury his bats in dung heaps over the winter to "keep them alive." It might have been late May before any teammate would closely follow him to the plate.

One of the most celebrated lines about Louisville Slugger bats was uttered by Vernon "Lefty" Gomez, a Hall of Fame pitcher with the New York Yankees. Gomez was not a man of undue modesty, but he once said of his .147 lifetime batting average: "The only time I ever broke a bat was when I backed out of the garage and ran over one."

Although Gomez may have been the standard-bearer for Famous Bat Stories, he was far from alone. Hillerich & Bradsby executive Frank Ryan remembered that Joe DiMaggio would take a fresh load of his bats to a delicatessen near Yankee Stadium to check their weights before putting them to work:

"Yeah, Louie, gimmie two pounds of ham, some potato salad and a Louisville Slugger."

Ryan also passed on the timeless story about Yankee catcher Yogi Berra and the bat label. Berra had complained his bat was "checking" (coming loose at the seams in the grain). He was told that was because he wasn't keeping the label of the bat "up"—the time-honored way of getting the best grain on the ball.

"I don't go up there to read," Berra explained.

To prevent checking, many players in the early days would "bone" their bats—rub a hard object, even bones, against them to tighten up the grain. Babe Ruth, as was the custom of the day, would first squirt warm tobacco juice on his bat, then rub it in with an empty pop bottle—perhaps only a slight improvement on the Eddie Collins school of bat protection.

Ruth—like every player since time immemorial—selected his favorite bat in some unexplainable and mystical fashion involving length, heft, balance, grain, "feel" and perhaps temperature, time of day and current wind speed.

One sportswriter told the story of Ruth examining more than 20 bats shipped to him at the Yankee training camp in St. Petersburg, Florida. Ruth spread the bats on the ground—each the same weight, length and style, each made of white ash. Ruth worked his way through the bats until he found the one—as he told the writer—"with some wood in it."

The Louisville Slugger worked its way into practically every corner of society—and the world. Every spring Hillerich & Bradsby would receive letters from managers of prison teams who were enthusiastic about the "new blood" at shortstop, or on the mound, the early pioneers of the no-cut contracts. The company received letters from all over the United States ad-

**Joe and Ted's Kiss.**
*Grateful sluggers Ted Williams and Joe DiMaggio kiss their bats in a Louisville Slugger ad.*

*Crack of the Bat: The Louisville Slugger Story*

# BONE RUBBED

## The Player's Own Finish

*The Finish the Players Give Their Own Bats, If Someone Else Doesn't Give It For Them*

*The Finish that Puts More Wallop In Every Hit*

## A New Selling Point for Louisville Sluggers

You've seen baseball players hone the surface of their bats with a dry meat bone, a horse shoe or a pop bottle, as Al Simmons is doing in the photograph above. Honing closes the pores of the bat, hardens its surface, prevents splintering and gives it greater resiliency, resulting in longer hits. Many players have requested us to finish their bats this way at the factory. For several years we have done so on special orders. Now, we have decided to give every Autographed Model Louisville Slugger this desirable bone-rubbed finish—without extra cost. Real bone is used in applying the finish and the result is far superior to that obtained by the player himself. HILLERICH & BRADSBY COMPANY, *Incorporated*, Manufacturers, Louisville, Ky.

*Now Applied to Autographed Models of Louisville Sluggers At the Factory*

## LOUISVILLE SLUGGER

 *Bats*

Bone Rubbed.
*The "bone rubbed" bats inspired more confidence, if not distance.*

dressed only to "The Bat Man" or "The Bat Factory" or "The Bat People" or "The Louisville Slugger."

Millions of Little Leaguers around the world used Louisville Sluggers. In 1964, the company received a letter from Sister Mary Xavier of the Alpha Girls' School in Kingston, Jamaica, offering thanks for the four dozen bats donated to its softball team.

"Please accept my deepest gratitude for your gift," she wrote. "Enclosed please find some snapshots of our girls' team. This is the group that won the Knockout Cup in the school competition. Isn't this a grand triumph for our first year in the sport?"

**Jamaica Sluggers.**
*Hillerich & Bradsby donated four dozen softball bats to the Alpha Girls School in Kingston, Jamaica, whose team promptly won the league title with them.*

Other amateurs enthusiastically endorsed the bat—and the game. The University of Louisville's photo archives has an old, grainy photograph of nuns playing baseball in an open field, a tableau of art, nature, natural order, religious order and a batting order.

In 1973, H&B helped re-create Civil War baseball history by shipping handmade, old-style bats to the Fort Pulaski National Monument at Savannah Beach, Georgia, where they were used as aids to encourage discussion about how sports were incorporated into garrison life in the 1860s; beans, bayonets and baseball.

Truly finicky Hillerich & Bradsby customers asked that their bats be measured in quarter-ounces and even eighth-ounces—weights that literally could vary, depending on how much humidity was sucked into the bats on a July night.

Willie Mays ordered bats weighing 34 $\frac{1}{8}$ ounces one year. The following year—apparently feeling a little stronger—he boosted the weight all the way to 34 $\frac{1}{2}$ ounces. St. Louis catcher-turned-broadcaster Tim McCarver ordered bats at 34 $\frac{1}{4}$ and 34 $\frac{1}{2}$ ounces, a difference that oculd almost be made up by adding another coat of lacquer.

It wasn't just ballplayers who got into the act. Jack McGrath, longtime vice president of marketing and public relations for Hillerich & Bradsby, was a much better golfer than baseball player. But he designed a wide-barreled bat with a tapering handle that officially became MC-44. Variations of it were eventually used by 50 players.

Speaking of non-baseball players, Michael Jordan used a Louisville Slugger during his brief career. His equipment lasted no longer than he did; the first shipment of bats featuring Jordan's name and "Chicago White Sox" on the barrel disappeared on its way to training camp.

Harry "The Hat" Walker, a National League batting champion with the St. Louis Cardinals in the 1940s, developed his own distinctive bat color pretty much on a whim. Walker was touring the H&B plant and noticed a bat in a bucket of dark stain, where it was being used as a stir stick. Walker pulled out the bat, said he liked the color, and the two-toned "Walker Finish"—still in use today as one of H&B's many bat finishes—was born.

Following somewhat the same color scheme, Eddie Collins—the guy who buried his bats in dung heaps—always insisted his bats be made of half-red and half-white timber, which included the "heart" of the wood. It's a good thing he never went into the perfume business.

**Nun Better.**
*The St. Catherine Dominican Sisters of Springfield, Kentucky, enjoy a pleasant afternoon of baseball.*

**The Walker.**
*The "Walker finish" bat comes in two colors—courtesy of Harry "The Hat" Walker.*

But not all the bats were selected for color—some required an audio component, too. Hugh Duffy, another Hall of Famer, who played for Chicago, Boston, Milwaukee and Philadelphia from 1888 to 1906, wanted his bats to "sound" right. The billets—the round wooden sticks used to make the bats—were bounced off the factory's concrete floor. Only those that produced the perfectly pitched "Duffy Ring" were used to turn his bats.

Baseball bats also went to war. During World War II, Louisville Sluggers found their way into a German prisoner-of-war camp in Upper Silesia. Dr. Carroll Witten of Louisville remembers that the POWs in his camp—many from Kentucky—cried when they saw the homegrown bats.

The first cruise missile fired by the *USS Louisville* nuclear attack submarine in the Persian Gulf War had the Louisville Slugger logo painted on its side—a genuine strike. Each of the sailors on board had received a personalized Louisville Slugger when the boat was commissioned.

But what might have been the most interesting military bat of all never got off the launching pad. In 1965, Hillerich & Bradsby began research into bombarding bats with atomic particles to irradiate the wood and make it tougher. Half a dozen bats were treated experimentally at the Lockheed Corp. facilities in Atlanta. Nothing came of it, except talk about "lighting up" a pitcher.

So personal did ballplayers take their bats, that when Jack McGrath retired in 1974, after 48 years with Hillerich & Bradsby, he wrote to many Hall of Fame players in search of bat stories he could use for a book.

McGrath, vice president of marketing and public relations, never found time to write his book, but his letters from the players remain on file in the University of Louisville archives. They are funny, interesting, poignant, sad and revealing.

Hank Greenberg, whose 58 home runs for the Detroit Tigers in 1938 came dangerously close to Babe Ruth's then untouchable 60, was always a tough negotiator on and off the field.

Greenberg, one of the few players to speak in more eloquent terms about his equipment, wrote that a baseball bat to a player was like a Stradivarius to a violinist.

He said he met with Bud Hillerich during the 1934 World Series to negotiate a personalized bat contract. That was an era long before player representatives, when players generally took what was offered in salary and fringe benefits and were happy with whatever they got.

Greenberg said he was not going to sell his signature for $25 or a set of Grand Slam golf clubs. He wanted $500, which Hillerich agreed to—after two hours of negotiations. Hillerich then paid Greenberg in cash—with 500 one-dollar bills.

Lloyd Waner was the "Little Poison" portion of the baseball-playing brothers who played for Pittsburgh in the 1930s, with his brother, Paul Waner, who was "Big Poison." Lloyd Waner told McGrath it was such a thrill to get bats with his name on them that he would hide them from the pitchers, who too often reduced them to kindling. Little Poison—aptly enough—preserved his bats with a mixture of tobacco juice and linseed oil, rubbing it in with an old bone.

The funniest letter came from Sandy Koufax, the fabulous Hall of Fame Los Angeles Dodger pitcher who told McGrath he appreciated being contacted, but as a lifetime .096 hitter, he had little to contribute to a book about bats.

Negro League star James "Cool Papa" Bell said he used Louisville Slugger bats for 29 years—most of them 35 inches long and weighing 38 and 39 ounces. Records from those leagues are incomplete, but what is known is that Bell had a lifetime .337 batting average. He told McGrath that most of the players in the Negro League used the company's bats.

As his nickname might imply, Charlie "The Mechanical Man" Gehringer was a model of consistency, leading American League second basemen in fielding for the Detroit Tigers nine times. He also led the league in hitting one year: 1937, when he hit .371.

**Down Under.**
*A bat made especially for members of the submarine* USS Louisville.

**Tiger Greats.**
*Hank Greenberg (third from left), joined by Charlie Gehringer, Rudy York and Birdie Tebbets, had his own way of negotiating bat contracts.*

In his letter to McGrath, Gehringer did grumble a bit that great fielders are never remembered as well as great hitters. Gehringer said he ordered six bats at a time, always looking for one with a big knot in the barrel, which made it harder.

Gehringer's first manager was Ty Cobb, who insisted that Gehringer use his bat model, a medium-slim bat that reminded Gehringer of a sword. Gehringer didn't especially like it, but was convinced that any Ty Cobb bat always contained the best possible ash—much better ash than any bat sent to Gehringer—so he used it.

Ty Cobb also wrote McGrath, asking if Hillerich & Bradsby had any of his old bats left in the factory. Cobb said the people in his hometown of Royston, Georgia, had created a museum in his honor, but he had little memorabilia left. McGrath wrote back, assuring Cobb that Hillerich & Bradsby would not "spare the horses" in finding some old bats—or making new ones.

A similar request came from Napoleon "Nap" Lajoie, a legendary player whose major league career lasted from 1896 to 1916. Two weeks later—after a bat had been sent to his home—Lajoie wrote to thank the company, adding he wanted to give his very best regards to all the boys.

**The Waners.**
*The Waner brothers, Lloyd and Paul, were taken on a company tour by a Hillerich & Bradsby executive.*

# MICKEY MANTLE

*KINGS OF SWING WHO MADE THE SLUGGERS SING*

*KINGS OF SWING WHO MADE THE SLUGGERS SING*

*KINGS OF SWING WHO MADE THE SLUGGERS SING*

*KINGS OF SWING WHO MADE THE SLUGGERS SING*

*KINGS OF SWING WHO MADE THE SLUGGERS SING*

In 1957, Yankee star Mickey Mantle wrote an instructional essay on "The Art of Batting" for the Hillerich & Bradsby Company. Mantle—who had won the Triple Crown (leading the league in batting average, home runs and runs batted in) in 1956—was among many Hall of Fame players who would write batting tips for the company. Others included Duke Snider, George Sisler and Tris Speaker.

Mantle's essay was interesting because it showed his human side—and a self-effacing sense of humor.

"When the Hillerich & Bradsby people asked me to jot down a few ideas about 'how to hit' I thought they were kidding. Now if it had been 'how to strike out' I would have been the perfect authority."

". . . What I'm trying to say is that a guy had better learn not to strike out too often if he ever wants to become a respectable hitter. Hitting the long ball or home run as I have done at times might make 'good copy,' as the sports writers yelp, but 'tape measure jobs' mean nothing without a degree of consistency.

"Sure, I'm tickled over the homers I've hit and I'd be lying if I didn't admit breaking Babe Ruth's record of 60 is my ambition, but I'm not kidding myself either. Ruth's '60' looks bigger every time I think about it and, frankly, I'd settle for another 52, my total in 1956."

Mantle went on to emphasize that just "meeting the ball" is the most important thing in hitting—and mentioned his tough times in doing it in his early years.

"But the pitchers, many of them anyway, completely fooled me during my first several years with the Yankees. Before I got 'temperamental' (according to the press) I'd sneak off in some corner and cry. That's right, bawl like a baby. I'll never forget the time I fanned five straight times during a double header in Boston.

"And were it not for Casey Stengel, who understood, and my late dad who bawled me out for crying like a baby, I'd probably be laboring in some Oklahoma lead mine. Dad gave it to me straight. He just let me have it and left it up to me. Thank the good Lord I had enough left in me to fight my way back to the Yankees after they sent me to Kansas City."

The Mick.
*Powerful Mickey Mantle takes a cut.*

# 5

*F I V E*

# FROM FOREST TO FIELD

*THE MAKING OF A LOUISVILLE SLUGGER*

Old Growth.
*White ash trees in old-growth forests were felled by hand in the early 1900s.*

t̲he very best white ash in the world grows in a 200-mile strip along the New York-Pennsylvania border, a wooded, rolling, mostly remote area blessed with just enough sun, just enough rain and just enough glacial till to make it happen.

Dick Reed, a logger for the Larimer & Norton Company, was kneeling before one of the trees on a low hill near Plattsburg, New York, a light snow floating down around him, his eyes measuring a place for the tree to fall. This is where Louisville Slugger baseball bats begin.

Like many who log in this area—and the loggers go back three and four generations—Reed is an inventive man. He has reworked the thick steel blade of his tractor—called a "skidder"—so it can move and tilt in eight directions. He has reworked the giant pincers behind the skidder so it can haul twice the number of logs from the woods as it was designed for—and do it while causing the least amount of damage possible.

Reed is self-employed, works from dawn to dusk, and owns about $500,000 worth of logging equipment, much of it homemade or home-modified. His investment is a long way from the good ol' days of logging, when a guy could operate with a pickup truck, chain saw, maul and wedge.

The economics—and difficulties—in cutting timber for baseball bats make it a unique operation. Of the 10 to 12 million board feet of ash lumber processed annually by Larimer & Norton, a wholly owned subsidiary of Hillerich & Bradsby, less than two percent of it—by volume—will become baseball bats.

Nothing is wasted. All of that board feet—and sawdust—gets used somewhere: baseball bats, tool handles, firewood, bedding for animals, furnace fuel or nursery mulch. The other prime outlet is in furniture stock: hard ash is often stained with an oak finish when it reaches the showroom.

As a rule, only 5-7 percent of the trees in these Pennsylvania-New York forests will be white ash. As a practical matter, other species—especially cherry and oak—will also be cut while the loggers are in the woods.

The process eats up a lot of wood. A triangular "split" of green ash about 40 inches long—the raw form from which a professional bat begins—will weigh about 20 pounds. A Ken Griffey Jr. bat—kiln-dried, shaped, sanded and finished in his favorite "Smith" black—will weigh 31 or 32 ounces. More than 18 pounds of wood will be removed in the process of shaping a single bat that weighs about two pounds.

That is a lot of hand labor just to manufacture each of the 200,000 professional-grade bats Hillerich & Bradsby makes each year—of which about 100,000 go to the major leagues. But there is no other way to maintain quality.

"The economics of it are scary," said Jack Norton, administrative manager for Hillerich & Bradsby and the son of one of the founders of Larimer & Norton.

After Dick Reed felled his quarry, dropping the 50-foot tree neatly into an opening about 15 feet wide on the snow-crusted forest floor, Norton

joined him to examine its grain. The grain is the heart of the wood business. For more than 100 years, baseball players have looked closely at their bats, running their hands along the grain, searching for imperfections, tiny knots and telltale chipping.

No two wooden bats—and Hillerich & Bradsby has made more than 100 million of them in its history—are exactly the same because no two trees are exactly the same. Some players prefer a wide-grained bat, some narrow—but almost all want the grain to run straight. In Jack Norton's eyes the best grain has about 6 to 10 growth rings per inch, with 8 rings being perfect.

Each ring represents one year's growth, which means it can take 25 to 30 consecutive good growing years for a tree to produce enough rings for a professional bat that's roughly three inches in diameter.

"Even then," said Norton, "only the first log from the lower 10 feet of the tree will make a good bat. You're getting into defects in the upper parts of the tree.

"See that bark?" he said, pointing to the upper trunk of a white ash. "See how it looks twisty? That's a sign the grain won't be straight, so there won't be any bats up there."

**Where It All Begins.** *Larimer & Norton employee, Dick Reed, drops a white ash on a snowy hillside.*

**On the Move.**
*Big tractors move the logs around the yard with huge pincers.*

**Woodpile.**
*Jack Norton stands before a 15-foot wall of logs.*

The logs are graded as they lie on the forest floor; only the best are allowed into the "bat stream" that will make its way to Louisville. The wood will be graded three more times, long before it becomes a Louisville Slugger.

Really good grain is so scarce that some trees might have only three or four professional bats in them—which might sell for $27 to $30 each. That same tree, if used for veneer, might bring in $3,000. But Hillerich & Bradsby is in the bat business.

The maddening part is there is little scientific proof that baseball bats with either wide, narrow or medium grain perform that much differently from one other. But in the eyes—and minds—of the customers, the professional ballplayers, grain matters.

"If the perception is there," said Norton, "we have to deal with it. It's a scramble, a struggle every year. The problem is that we have to go through that 10 to 12 million feet of ash logs every year to get that professional bat so that whenever Tony Gywnn wants to go to the plate he's got a nice bat to use.

Junie Hillerich, who took over as company president after his brother, Ward, died in 1949, led the firm into the timber business. Before that, Hillerich & Bradsby bought wood from Indiana, Kentucky and Canada, as well as

Pennsylvania and New York. Some white ash was purchased in the South—especially during World War II—but southern ash grows more quickly, is lighter and not as strong.

"Basically," said Jack Norton. "It came down to the company getting a little smarter. OK, the better ash is coming from here so we better get focused . . . . We better control the spot."

In 1952, Hillerich & Bradsby bought a small mill near Akeley, New York, from two men named Irv Norton and Danny Larimer. The mill's beginnings just after World War II were so humble that Norton and his family lived nearby in a tent, barely staying one step ahead of the bill collectors. It took a timely infusion of $2,000 in cash from Larimer to save the whole business from bankruptcy.

Over the years Hillerich & Bradsby bought a mill in Troy, Pennsylvania, then others in Ellicottville, New York, Galeton, Pennsylvania, and Hancock, New York. This expansion stitched together a neat pattern of sawmills and holding yards that assured that the Louisville bat operation would maintain an adequate supply of timber. Most of the mills had been family owned and operated. Most family members stayed on—as have their descendants.

**Year-round Process.**
*Heavy machines move the billets from place to place in the snow.*

Hillerich & Bradsby owns about 8,000 acres of timber in the area—which would barely supply two weeks' worth of timber a year for its bats. Its other sources cam from private landowners, loggers, various corporations and certain state and federal forests where controlled logging is allowed. The company has two foresters who tend its land, monitor logging operations, mark trees for cutting and continually search for other sources of ash.

The overall supply of ash remains ample, but the worldwide market for the wood fluctuates; a sudden Japanese interest in ash always creates concern. The boom in aluminum bats has helped protect the forests; Hillerich & Bradsby now produces about a million wooden bats a year, way down from the seven million bats it made in the early 1970s. But the demand for the very best wood for its professional bats has actually gone up, so the search for the best timber is endless.

Of that one million bats, about 700,000 are made in its Ellicottville, New York, plant, which was a bat-making operation when the company bought it in 1963. The Ellicottville bats are not of professional quality; the best timber always goes to Louisville.

The Ellicottville market consists of discount stores, Little Leagues and other youth leagues that still use wooden bats. The factory makes bats for special promotions at baseball parks and also for corporate events and related markets. It also manufactures about 750,000 of the 14-inch mini-bats used for thousands of advertisers and special events—including a Bat Out of Hell for the singer Meat Loaf. It makes the mini-bats given away at the Louisville Slugger Museum.

It also produced the company's first aluminum bats—before Hillerich & Bradsby bought an aluminum bat company in California. Its first manager, Babe Gleockler, came from Akeley. Two of his daughters still work in Ellicottville. One of them is so loyal to her product that when her son played high school baseball, she insisted he use a wooden bat—a single piece of ash in an aluminum forest.

Hillerich & Bradsby now owns half a dozen mills or storage areas, which employ about 120 people. One of them, a modern facility in Galeton, Pennsylvania, produces only "dimension lumber" for the manufacture of furniture. The company's vintage operation is at Troy, Pennsylvania, where 10-foot ash logs sent by men like Dick Reed are cut into smaller 40-inch "bolts," then divided into the triangular "splits" for processing.

"It's an interesting operation," said Norton. "To me it's the heart and soul of the bat business. If you take away the hydraulic splitter and put a guy out in the woods, it's exactly the way they did it, and have done it, for 100 years."

The Troy operation is perched on a bare hillside, farm fields and wood lots flowing away from it in all directions. White ash logs about 14 to 20 inches in diameter are stacked above it in uneven piles 20 feet high. A roaring loader carries the logs to the back of a small frame building, where they are fed toward a huge, whining saw blade that neatly cuts them into the 40-inch bolts.

The bolts of wood are placed upright on the floor, narrow end up. Ash is a wood that splits evenly, but it must first be marked. A round piece of metal about the size of a can of tuna is laid on the butt of the bolt. A worker draws a series of circles on the white wood—each circle about the diameter of the barrel end of a bat. A small wedge is pounded into the wood between the circles, providing a tiny crack that will help guide the 10-ton hydraulic splitter.

**First the Bolt . . .**
*Logs are split into bolts inside a vintage mill in Troy, Pennsylvania.*

The bolt is then slid under the splitter, its flat blade jamming down into the crack. In seconds, the circular piece of ash is split almost perfectly in half, its grain yielding to the relentless steel. That half is split, then split again, until—as in slicing a pie—the whole has been divided into triangular pieces. Depending on the original diameter of the tree, anywhere from four to eight bat-sized "splits" will be cleaved from a 40-inch bolt.

"In the old days," said Norton, "the loggers would go out, cut down the trees and make the splits right there in the woods."

At Troy, the triangular pieces are fed into a "roughing" lathe, its 45 sharp knives attacking the split at 3,300 rpm. The lathe rounds off the triangular split in seconds, hurling bark and sawdust into a storage area. The sound is deafening, a jet-engine-level whine competing with a radio turned up to full blast in a futile effort to overcome the sound of the lathe.

The finished product—a rounded piece of ash called a "billet"—is graded again. The poorest will be sent through a "dowel" machine—which cuts the billet's diameter to 2 $^{11}/_{16}$ inches. They will be sent to Ellicottville for use in promotional bats. The best—about 30 to 45 percent—will be shipped to a company mill at Akeley.

The Akeley mill, under the direction of Jeff Eckman, is continually reinventing and rebuilding itself. Akeley has four air-dried kilns. It has a pair of "tubesaws" that literally bore out billets from the ash logs. Almost all the Akeley design and construction was done by its employees; Jack Norton's father first developed the tubesaw.

The billets are dried to about 12 to 15 percent moisture, less than half what it was in the woods. Once out of the kiln, the wood is again inspected.

**Then the Splitter. . .**
*The bolts are neatly sectioned by a splitter.*

The best billets are trimmed down to 37 inches in length, 2 and $^{27}/_{32}$ inch in diameter, and shipped to Louisville. Those not making the grade—like ballplayers who are not quite up to major league play—are shipped to Ellicottville.

Because every tree is different, billets of the exact same dimension vary greatly in weight. The ones sent to Louisville can weigh anywhere from 84 to 102 ounces—about five or six pounds. Norton said he has seen 25- to 30-ounce differences in the same-sized pieces of wood.

"But almost all of them will come out weighing about 32 to 33 ounces as finished bats," he said.

Once at the Hillerich & Bradsby factory in Louisville, the billets are again inspected—this time by the men who make the bats. It's a process that hasn't changed much since the 1880s, when Bud Hillerich turned the very first bats in a small, red-brick building in downtown Louisville.

In the old days, the raw wood often would arrive in the triangular splits, or in four-inch-square pieces. They were air-dried in massive company yards for 12 to 18 months before being processed. Occasionally, ballplayers would bring in their own wood, looking for somebody to turn a bat.

Chances were very good they would meet a bat maker named Bickel. Henry Bickel began with the company in 1881 and worked there for 57 years. His son, Fritz Bickel, began working at Hillerich & Bradsby in 1912 at age 14. He earned $3.75 a week—and considered himself well paid.

**Anniversary Celebration.**
*Two veterans of the 1880s, Henry "Pa" Bickel (left) and J. A. "Bud" Hillerich Sr., cross bats in celebration of the 60th anniversary of the company.*

# STAN MUSIAL

*KINGS OF SWING WHO MADE THE SLUGGERS SING*

*KINGS OF SWING WHO MADE THE SLUGGERS SING*

*KINGS OF SWING WHO MADE THE SLUGGERS SING*

*KINGS OF SWING WHO MADE THE SLUGGERS SING*

*KINGS OF SWING WHO MADE THE SLUGGERS SING*

No baseball player in history has ever suffered a more fortunate injury than Stan "The Man" Musial, who began his baseball career as a 17-year-old pitcher. Filling in for an outfielder, he made a diving catch and hurt his left shoulder. It ended his days as a pitcher and began the story of one of baseball's greatest hitters.

One year later—after beginning that 1941 season in Class C ball—he hit .426 in the month of September for the St. Louis Cardinals. He would spend another 21 years in a Cardinal uniform, batting a lifetime .331, most of it with a Louisville Slugger in his hands.

"I had the thinnest bat in the major leagues," Musial said. "I made my bat with a Babe Ruth handle and a Jimmie Foxx barrel and I would scrape down the handle to make it even thinner.

"I never used tar and I didn't like wax. I'd scrape up the handle a little bit so I could hold it better."

Musial, who had 3,630 lifetime hits, was so consistent, he had 1,815 of them at home and 1,815 on the road. His compressed, left-handed batting stance was as familiar to baseball fans as hot dogs and doubleheaders. He quickly learned that using a light bat—33 ounces, 34 $\frac{1}{2}$ inches—was the best way to be an effective hitter. He would drop the bat's weight to about 31 ounces by the end of the season, very light for the era—1941 to 1963—in which he played.

"It was amazing," he said. "In those days I could pick up a bat and tell you exactly what it weighed: 33, 32, 31 ounces."

Musial was so young—20—when he signed a contract with Hillerich & Bradsby that it had to be redone when he became 21, a legal adult. It was—he remembered—for about $100.

"I liked a wide-grain bat," he said. "It was more solid to me than a thin-grained bat.

"I used to just give them to anybody at the end of the season. I let my friends have them. The clubhouse manager always got me some more good ones."

Musial—who was laughing at the memory of it—said he always had a good supply of bats unless the Brooklyn Dodgers were in town.

"When the Dodgers came to town I'd always be missing a few bats," he said. "You know who it was; Pee Wee Reese and Rube Walker. They told me years later they'd take my bats so I couldn't use them against the Dodgers."

Stan the Man.
*Stan Musial's classic swing.*

ROYAL PHOTO CO.
LOUISVILLE, KY.

**A Famous Visitor.**
*Ted Williams was a frequent visitor to the plant—always searching for just the right bats.*

Fritz Bickel worked at Hillerich & Bradsby for 50 years, making bats for Ty Cobb, Tris Speaker, Casey Stengel and Lou Gehrig, eventually becoming foreman of the bat department. He would remember the time he worked all night making bats for Babe Ruth, who was due to visit the plant the next day. Bickel carefully laid out the bats. Ruth walked in, picked them up by the knob one at a time and let them drop to the hard floor, listening to the ring.

"They aren't worth a damn," Ruth said, walking away.

Bud Hillerich later told Bickel that Ruth had been kidding; he wanted the bats. The year was 1927, the year Ruth hit 60 home runs with them.

Augie Bickel, nephew of Henry Bickel, worked for Hillerich & Bradsby for 42 years, from 1931 to 1973. Augie Bickel would think so much of his job—and the company—he would build a museum in the basement of his home. He filled it with old bats, photographs, news clippings and the tools he had used to make bats, tools his father had made for him. Augie Bickel had started at $13 a week.

"I got so I could make bats just by feeling them with my hands," Bickel said.

He is a small man, 5 feet 4 inches tall and never weighing much more than 128 pounds. He worked in an old brick building that was impossibly

*Crack of the Bat: The Louisville Slugger Story*

Tall Stacks.
Millions of billets would be stacked for years
to be air-dried.

**Lathe.**
*A noisy, churning lathe (left) turns a split into a rounded billet.*

**Tube Saw.**
*Some billets are carved directly from bolts by a tube saw (right)—this one at a mill in Akeley, New York.*

overcrowded, jammed from its wooden floors to exposed ceilings with timber racks, billets and bats. The lathes and grinders were turned by belts that ran overhead. Wood shavings were sucked into pipes that ran back into the boiler room, where they were burned for fuel.

Even then, most of the Louisville Slugger bats were made on automatic lathes; preset knives could turn out hundreds of any model a day. But the very best of them—the ones that had the number 125 on them signifying top-quality major league bats—were turned by hand.

When an order came in—say from Joe DiMaggio—a model of the bat DiMaggio used would be taken from the thousands of models kept in a company vault. Bickel would place that bat in front of him, almost duplicating it just from sight. Using hand tools that would delicately pare away wood as the billet spun on the lathe before him, he would "rough out" the shape, use a "knob tool" to shape the handle, then use calipers to finish the job. It would take him about 15 minutes to craft each bat.

"I had to hold my calipers in one hand and my tools in the other," he said. "I'd caliper all the way down the bat, then slough it off.

"I could feel it. I could put my calipers over the turning bat, then check it with the model one. I could just feel when it was right."

In time, Hillerich & Bradsby developed an elaborate card system for tracking the thousands of models of bats. Each player's name was listed on a card—with the date and number of his order. Other named cards were used to track the size of the bats.

The company also began stamping model numbers on the bats to help keep track of them. The system was based on the first letter of the player's last name. Babe Ruth's bat model, for instance, was R-43; he was the 43rd player with a last name beginning in "R" to have a bat model named for him. Ted Williams used a W-148. With some of the more common names—like Brown—a player might have a B-378.

Honus Wagner
Old-time ballplayers such as
Honus Wagner (left) often
visited the Louisville factory.

**J Models.**
*The ends of bats were stamped with the initial of a player's last name.*

But players might also use a bat made popular by another player. One of the most popular bats of all time—an S-2 model—was used by Willie Mays, Eddie Mathews and Ernie Banks. But it was first made for Vern Stephens—who batted .286 with it in a good, but not great, 15-year career. Mickey Mantle used his version of a K-55 which was first used by Chuck Klein, who hit 300 career home runs, including 43 in 1929.

Hall of Famer George Brett used a T-85—a bat first made for the lovably hapless "Marvelous Marv" Throneberry. Hank Aaron used an A-99—but it was very similar to Babe Ruth's R-43. One of the most popular modern bats was an M-110—with which Eddie Malone batted .257 in an 86-game major league career with the Chicago White Sox in 1949 and 1950. Modern-day slugger Ken Griffey Jr. uses a C-271, a legally "cupped" bat with the ash scooped away from the top of the barrel. The model was first used by Jose Cardenal, who hit 138 home runs in 18 years.

Except for special occasions in the Louisville Slugger Museum, no one at Hillerich & Bradsby turns bats by hand. Modern bats have achieved such conformity—shorter, lighter, easier to swing—only 40 to 50 models are produced on a regular basis, although they are still spread among hundreds of ballplayers.

Now, the bats are formed on modern lathes that use metal templates—the company has about 270 in stock for various orders—or preset knives. The rounded billets—inspected one more time to ensure a good grain—are cut into bats in 10 to 15 seconds.

Danny Luckett, 51, is one of only three men remaining at Hillerich & Bradsby who can still turn a bat by hand, the last descendants of a line of craftsmen dating to the 1880s. One of the men who taught Luckett to turn a bat was Augie Bickel.

**Inspection.**
*A Hillerich & Bradsby executive inspects billets sent to Louisville from New York and Pennsylvania.*

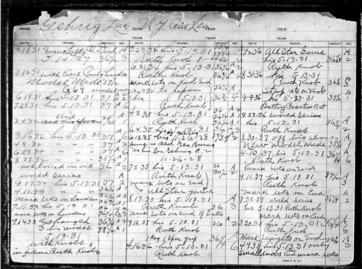

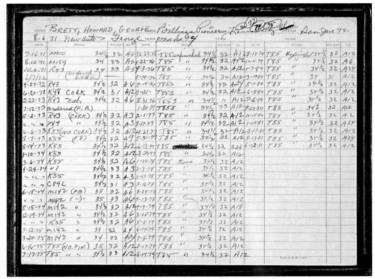

Luckett has been with Hillerich & Bradsby for 30 years. Like a ballplayer working his way into the major leagues, Luckett first learned the craft while turning college bats, worked his way to minor league bats, then to major league bats. "It took six to eight months," he said.

Standing before a hand-turning lathe, Luckett demonstrated his skill turning a C-243, originally a Rod Carew-model bat. Luckett is standing in a modern factory, air-conditioned, well-lighted and OSHA-enhanced, but still filled with the sweet, unmistakable smell of sawdust and the shrill whine of woodworking machinery. What's most apparent is that the turning of a bat by hand hasn't changed since horse-drawn carts were parked outside the old Louisville factory. How else to do it?

With an old C-243 as a guide, Luckett wrapped his finger around a spinning billet, gently pressing a shaping knife against the wood with his

**Bat Cards.**

*For 75 years, order and bat dimensions were handwritten on individual cards. Shown here (clockwise from top left) are cards for Henry Aaron, Lou Gehrig, George Brett and Joe DiMaggio.*

Yesterday . . .
*As illustrated by Pa Bickel,*
*the technique of hand-turning a bat*
*has changed little in 100 years.*

And Hand–Turning Today . . .
*Danny Luckett is one of the few men*
*in the world who can still turn a bat*
*by hand.*

thumb. He slowly moved his hand along the bat, wood shavings piling up on his arms, constantly checking his work with calipers against the taper and thickness of the Carew bat.

Behind him a "Defiance" lathe is loudly eating its way through white-ash billets, turning out a bat every 15 to 20 seconds, its preset knives every bit as precise as Luckett's thumb. It will take Luckett 15 minutes to turn one of his bats. There's no need to ask which one Rod Carew would have preferred.

But modern major league baseball players rarely visit the Hillerich & Bradsby factory. They are content with what the company sends them; the great majority still swing a Louisville Slugger.

*Crack of the Bat: The Louisville Slugger Story*

When Luckett gets an order for a few dozen bats for a player, he will first select only one billet from a particular weight grouping. He will turn that bat in the preset machine lathe, with information on a player's size and weight preference now stored in computers. If that bat matches what the player wants, Luckett will machine-turn the rest of the order using only billets from that weight group.

Once turned, the bats are sent to a belt-sander to smooth the cut marks left by the lathe. After that, they are branded with the Louisville Slugger logo—a logo that has evolved into a more modern shape over the years to better fit all Hillerich & Bradsby products—not just its bats.

With most bats, the logo is burned into the wood, a satisfying process that gives the bats a more vintage look; there's something about smoke gently curling up from wood that fulfills the sense of baseball history. Other bats will have logos embossed in foil later in the production process, especially the sleeker, all-black bats of the modern athletes.

After the bats are burn-branded, they are again sanded to smooth the burned edges of the logo. The tiny nubs at the end of the bats are trimmed away, and the rough ends are sanded. What's left is a bat of pure, natural white ash, ready for any of the almost dozen finishes ballplayers prefer.

The finish seals the wood, protects it, makes it stronger and adds a decorative touch. For many years, there were only three ways a player might want a bat: with no finish at all, dipped in natural lacquer or flame tempered, briefly putting the bat into fire to seal the wood.

New processes and color schemes have moved into the game, expanding the possibilities. Some "composite" bats are now fully dipped in fiberglass, which gives them a solid protective coat.

**Old Branding . . .**
*All bats were once branded with a big wheel.*

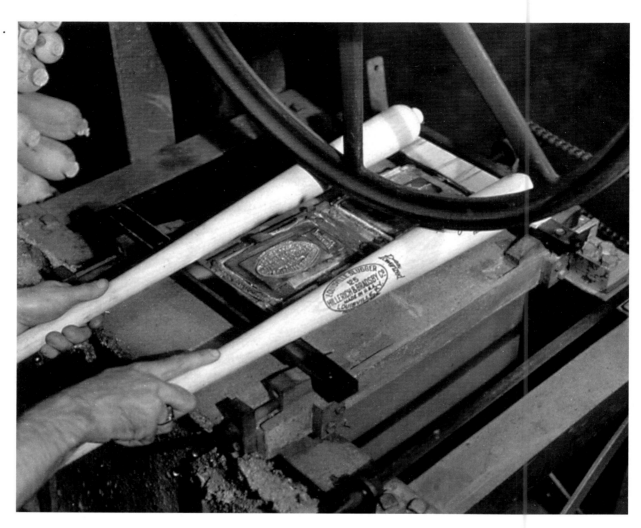

All-black bats have become popular. Ken Griffey Jr. prefers a "Smith" finish—all black and dipped in urethane. Tony Gwynn prefers a "Gwynn" model, with a black barrel and no finish on the handle.

Other bat models include a "Butler," which has a brown barrel with no finish on the handle, a dark-brown "Hickory" finish and, more recently, a "Galen" finish, a pale, rose hue about the color of spilled red wine.

Luckett said he is aware that the product he makes is special, and he still takes pride in making the Louisville Slugger. "I know if I made somebody some bats," he said, "and I know if they're going to be on television, I watch to be sure they're using our bats."

**New Branding . . .**
*Modern branding is done much more efficiently.*

*Crack of the Bat: The Louisville Slugger Story*

The Flame.
*Flame tempering a bat helps seal the grain.*

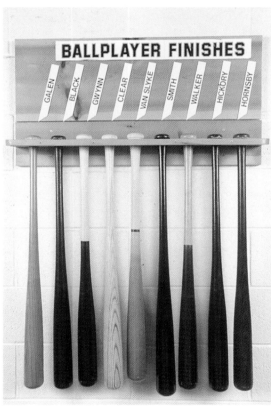

BALLPLAYER FINISHES

GALEN  BLACK  GWYNN  CLEAR  VAN SLYKE  SMITH  WALKER  HICKORY  HORNSBY

Finishes.
*Nine different bat finishes are required by today's major leaguers.*

# DEREK JETER

*KINGS OF SWING WHO MADE THE SLUGGERS SING*

*KINGS OF SWING WHO MADE THE SLUGGERS SING*

*KINGS OF SWING WHO MADE THE SLUGGERS SING*

*KINGS OF SWING WHO MADE THE SLUGGERS SING*

Shortstop sensation Derek Jeter is already banging on the front door of the shrine reserved for other New York Yankee legends, and he's done it swinging a Louisville Slugger in every at-bat of his major league career. He's had to fight the urge to switch bats—as does every major league player—but he's held firm.

My thinking is: "If it ain't broke, don't fix it,' " Jeter said.

Nothing's been broken yet. Jeter came out of a Kalamazoo (Michigan) high school in 1992 labeled the National High School Player of the Year. He played 15 games at shortstop for the Yankees in 1995, then was named American League Rookie of the Year in 1996. But—as with all modern players—there was a lot of adjustment going from the aluminum bats used in Little League and high school to the white ash of the professionals.

"I'd heard of Louisville Slugger, but didn't know too much about it," he said. "I went to a few tryouts in high school and had to use wooden bats. I started using a P-72 model (34 inches, 32 ounces) because I liked its feel. It was slim, like an aluminum bat, and felt about the same when I swung it."

Indeed, millions of young baseball players had grown up using only aluminum bats, which created a loss of identity for the traditional wooden Louisville Slugger bats the company had to work years to overcome. The aluminum bats produced more "pop," so much so that all of professional baseball's hallowed records would have been in instant jeopardy had its use spread into the major leagues.

But Jeter also noticed a difference between the aluminum and wooden bats that was a little more subtle. Except in the hands of incredibly powerful hitters such as Mark McGwire and Sammy Sosa, a baseball had to be hit on the "sweet spot" with a wooden bat if it was to jump off the bat. With aluminum, the ball had a tendency to jump off the bat from a lot of places.

"I didn't notice any loss of power or distance with the wooden bat as much as I noticed the wooden bat has a lot less room for error," he said.

Jeter learned quickly. He hit 19 homers in 1998, but in 1999, at 6-foot-3 and 195 pounds, up 15 pounds from his rookie season, he batted .349 with 24 home runs and 102 RBIs. In four full seasons of major league play, he's compiled a .318 batting average, played on three World Series-championship teams and been named an All-Star in 1998 and 1999—a tradition that should continue for a long time.

Jeter, who estimates that more than half the Yankees use Louisville Sluggers, said many players will begin using a lighter bat at the end of the season, but he sticks with his P-72.

"For me it's being in a comfort zone," he said. "I have great confidence with it."

As with most ballplayers, Jeter is not paid a lot of money to use the Louisville Slugger; it's often just a few hundred dollars and a set of new golf clubs. He views it as a craftsman finding the best tools possible, then using them to his advantage.

"I don't sit around and worry that I don't get paid for something that really helps me out," he said. "The bat you use helps you make the money."

A Yank.
*Derek Jeter*

# SIX

# "BLACK BETSY" AND OTHER BATS OF THE RICH, FAMOUS AND INFAMOUS

**Notches.**
*Babe Ruth carved 21 notches in this bat, one for each home run, in 1927, the year he hit 60 home runs.*

**a**s baseball rockets into the new millennium, the escalating value of its old bats has now reached that lofty point where the white ash swung by the game's vintage stars far exceeds the money they earned while swinging it.

If the bats have a player's decal on them—an advertising promotion used by Hillerich & Bradsby in the early 1900s—then so much the better.

One example would be the heavyweight bat (an R-43) swung by Babe Ruth in 1927, the year he hit 60 home runs. That bat—with 21 gunslinger-like notches in its Louisville Slugger label signifying home runs he hit that year—is one of the featured attractions in the Louisville Slugger Museum.

Early in the year 2000, that 1927 bat was valued at $100,000 by collector Dave Bushing, the owner of Vintage Sports Equipment of Libertyville, Illinois. Bushing had valued the bat at $75,000 only a year earlier.

It wasn't until 1930 that Ruth earned $80,000, a figure that sticks in the mind because that was the year President Herbert Hoover earned a mere $75,000, and Ruth supposedly said: "Yeah, well I had a better year than he did."

Bushing, a veteran collector who appraised all the bats in the Slugger museum before it opened, said he has sold a Babe Ruth bat for $94,000. The bat was from the 1931 season, when Ruth hit .373 and clubbed 46 home runs.

"That bat was game-used," Bushing said. "It had been autographed to some guy and there were all kinds of photos documenting the event. The new owner got all the photos, too. It's part of the package."

Bushing said he sold two game-used Ty Cobb bats with excellent documentation, one for $42,000, the other for $53,000. A "run-of-the-mill"—but game-used—Lou Gehrig bat might sell for $35,000 to $40,000. The bat collectors' market—as with all memorabilia business—has a lot to do with being in the right place at the right time.

"I sold a Mel Ott bat for $7,200, bought it back for $8,000, and two weeks later sold it for $10,000," he said.

The bat-collecting business generally divides itself into bats used before and after World War II. The most valuable are those Bushing called "side-written" bats—pre-World War II bats with a player's name written with a grease pencil on the side.

"Before the war," Bushing said, "when a player cracked a bat and returned it to Louisville, a guy named Bill Morrow would write the date, and the player that shipped the bat, on its side.

"H&B would keep that bat in its vault. Then the company could use that bat as a model to make the replacement bat. In terms of guaranteeing a certain player used a bat, a side-written bat is as good as it gets. The name is right there.

"We sold a side-written bat returned to H&B in August 1938 by Joe DiMaggio for $36,000. It would be worth $55,000 to $60,000 now."

The "side-written" bats were often returned to Hillerich & Bradsby in the most interesting of fashions; players would just stick a label on the side

of the broken bat, pay the postage and stick it in the mail. "We got a lot of bats that way," said company executive Rex Bradley. One such bat kept in the company's storage area was a Wally Schang model that was used by a ball player named Jeff Heath. Schang had batted .234 in a major league career that lasted from 1913 to 1931, when he played on five teams. Heath batted .293 for 10 years in the 1930s and '40s, most of that time spent with Cleveland.

Bushing said the "holy grail" of bats are the pre-1921 "Shoeless" Joe Jackson models turned by Hillerich & Bradsby. Those bats became rare for all the wrong reasons. Jackson's participation in the 1919 Chicago "Black Sox" scandal—and the degree of his involvement is still argued—got him banned from baseball.

Jackson's admirers included Babe Ruth and Ty Cobb. He batted .356 lifetime—trailing only Cobb (.367) and Rogers Hornsby (.358). But Jackson's career was foreshortened at 13 years, meaning there were fewer bats bearing his name. And the rarity of a Jackson bat enhances its value.

"It was called a "Black Betsy," Bushing said. "It was actually dark brown, probably stained with tobacco juice. It was 36 inches long and weighed 40 ounces. A nice one might go for $125,000."

From about 1916 until about 1920, Hillerich & Bradsby also put full-color decals on bats for promotional use. They appeared on bat models used by Honus Wagner, Frank "Home Run" Baker, Tris Speaker, Ty Cobb and Christy Mathewson, as well as—of course—"Shoeless" Joe Jackson.

A bat collector named Bob Rogers of Lansing, Michigan, said Hillerich & Bradsby offered "mini-bats" with decals on them, as well as full-sized bats. The bat's worth depends mostly on the condition of the decal, but Rogers said the mini-bats could sell for from $1,500 to $3,000, with the larger bats worth at least $500 more. A full-sized bat with decal would sell for at least $8,000, especially models made for Honus Wagner, Ty Cobb and Joe Jackson.

**Side-written Bats.**
*Players wanting replacement bats just wrote their names on the sides of their broken bats and mailed them back to the factory.*

Decals.
*(Clockwise from top left) Honus Wagner, Ty Cobb, Jake Daubert, Frank Baker, and Nap Lajoie.*

*Crack of the Bat: The Louisville Slugger Story*

Hillerich & Bradsby also produced thousands of mini-bats bearing players' signatures; bats which were also used to commemorate special events—a practice that continues today. The company's plant makes—and stamps—about 750,000 of the miniature bats a year, including almost 250,000 to be given away annually to visitors to the Louisville Slugger Museum.

Many of those, too, have become collectors' items. For example, Rogers said, a miniature bat made to commemorate the infamous George Brett "pine tar" incident—a mini-bat with imitation pine tar on its handle—might now be worth $25 to $30.

Bat collecting is tricky because of the difficulty in documenting game-used bats, especially after 1950 or so. About that time, Hillerich & Bradsby went to a card-file system to keep track of players rather than writing their names on returned bats.

Many books have been written to help collectors, including one titled *Bats* by Vince Malta, Ronald Fox, Bill Riddell and Michael Specht. It lists the best ways to search for old bats. Among its pointers:

Check a supposedly game-used bat for identifying marks. That would include teeth or track marks where the lace of a ball indents a bat; a round indentation where a ball hits the white ash of a bat; or a roundish mud mark from a dirty ball.

Bats used since the 1980s also have telltale "ink marks." American League balls leave a blue lettering mark; National League balls leave black ink marks. The better, most consistent hitters leave bat marks all their own: Will Clark and Wade Boggs typically have ink marks concentrated just below their names.

Some collectors' work is worthy of Sherlock Holmes. Serious collectors know, for example, that Harmon Killebrew was notorious for using a lot of pine tar. Mickey Mantle consistently spread his pine tar from 8 to 12 inches along the bat. Cal Ripken Jr.'s bats can be identified by cleat marks near the barrel, where he would bang away the mud from his spikes. Jackie Robinson would cut off the last three-quarters of an inch of his bat to make it lighter—a precursor to the cupped bat—making him a pioneer in another area, too.

**Pine Tar Special.**
*A replica of the George Brett "pine tar" bat.*

**Mantle's Bat Card.**

*The card on which Mickey Mantle's orders and bat dimensions were kept.*

The selling of vintage bats on computer websites also has boomed in recent years, but Vintage Sports guru Dave Bushing warns against the many fraudulent producers to be found on-line.

"There's a lot of pirates out there," he said. "It's like the wild west. I've seen all sorts of bats that were altered or doctored to be made to look old. Buyers must be sure they know what they're getting before buying anything.

"They should ask for "feedbacks" from other customers who have dealt with a particular dealer, and always put their money in escrow until they can examine the product."

*Crack of the Bat: The Louisville Slugger Story*

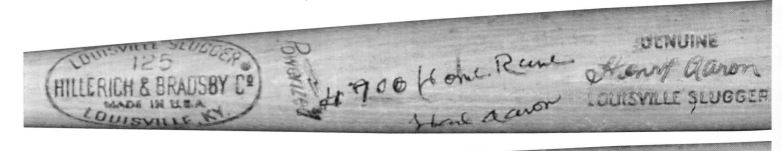

Legendary Sluggers.
*Bats used by Hank
Aaron, Johnny Bench,
George Brett.*

# KEN GRIFFEY JR.

*KINGS OF SWING WHO MADE THE SLUGGERS SING*

*KINGS OF SWING WHO MADE THE SLUGGERS SING*

*KINGS OF SWING WHO MADE THE SLUGGERS SING*

*KINGS OF SWING WHO MADE THE SLUGGERS SING*

*KINGS OF SWING WHO MADE THE SLUGGERS SING*

Ken Griffey Jr.'s return to the Cincinnati Reds for the 2000 baseball season brings his career—and that of his father, Ken Griffey Sr.—full circle. "Junior," as he is known to baseball legions, was a star in Cincinnati youth leagues, while his father played for the Reds. Junior played football at fabled Moeller High School, where he was such a great running back, the University of Oklahoma—among others—offered him a scholarship.

But baseball was in his blood, and two years after being the first player picked in the 1987 amateur draft he was carrying a Louisville Slugger up to the plate for the Seattle Mariners, where, at age 19, he batted .264 with 16 home runs and, of course, doubled in his first major league at-bat. Hillerich & Bradsby player representative Chuck Schupp remembers sitting in a dugout with the 19-year-old Griffey signing the 20-year contract to use Louisville Slugger bats. He recalls that the young Griffey quipped, "One of my goals in life is to outlast my 20-year contract." And it seems that he just might do that.

Probably the finest natural hitter in the game today, Griffey used his Louisville Slugger, the C-271 Jose Cardenal model 34 in., 31 oz., black double-lacquer bat, to hit 398 home runs in 11 major league seasons, including 209 from 1996 to 1999. In 1990, he and his father became the first-ever father-and-son combination to play major league baseball on the same team.

The Hillerich & Bradsby Co. plans a Louisville Slugger ad featuring Ken Griffey Sr., Ken Griffey Jr. and perhaps the next generation of Griffey excellence, Junior's son Trey.

Griffey's return to Cincinnati, where his father starred on the Big Red Machine with Johnny Bench, Pete Rose, Joe Morgan and others, has sparked hopes that history might fully repeat itself in Cincinnati. It's also good news right down the road in Louisville, whose AAA affiliate, the Louisville RiverBats, has the Reds as a new parent club and is ready to open a new ballpark, Louisville Slugger Field.

Now a Red.
*Ken Griffey Jr.*

# THE SILVER BAT AWARD

One of the most prestigious individual awards in sports is the "Silver Bat," which is presented annually to the batting champions of both the American League and the National League.

The award was first presented to the major league batting champions in 1949. George Kell of the Detroit Tigers and Jackie Robinson of the Brooklyn Dodgers were the first recipients. Actually, the trophy had been awarded to the minor league batting champions from 1934 to 1948. At one time, it had been known as the "Louisville Slugger Trophy."

Along with the Silver Bat, each champion also receives the John A. "Bud" Hillerich Memorial Award. It is a sheepskin certificate created in 1946, upon the death of the man credited for launching the success of Louisville Slugger.

The Silver Bat is silver plated in sterling and weighs approximately 56 ounces. It is 34 inches long and is engraved with the player's autograph and the vital statistics of his winning accomplishments. An official of Hillerich & Bradsby presents the award at the player's home stadium during the following season.

## LOUISVILLE SLUGGER "SILVER BAT" WINNERS

### AMERICAN LEAGUE

| Year | Name |
|---|---|
| 1949 | George Kell (Detroit) |
| 1950 | Billy Goodman (Boston) |
| 1951 | Ferris Fain (Philadelphia) |
| 1952 | Ferris Fain (Philadelphia) |
| 1953 | Mickey Vernon (Washington) |
| 1954 | Bobby Avila (Cleveland) |
| 1955 | Al Kaline (Detroit) |
| 1956 | Mickey Mantle (New York) |
| 1957 | Ted Williams (Boston) |
| 1958 | Ted Williams (Boston) |
| 1959 | Harvey Kuenn (Detroit) |
| 1960 | Pete Runnels (Boston) |
| 1961 | Norman Cash (Detroit) |
| 1962 | Pete Runnels (Boston) |
| 1963 | Carl Yastrzemski (Boston) |
| 1964 | Tony Oliva (Minnesota) |
| 1965 | Tony Oliva (Minnesota) |
| 1966 | Frank Robinson (Baltimore) |
| 1967 | Carl Yastrzemski (Boston) |
| 1968 | Carl Yastrzemski (Boston) |
| 1969 | Rod Carew (Minnesota) |
| 1970 | Alex Johnson (California) |
| 1971 | Tony Oliva (Minnesota) |
| 1972 | Rod Carew (Minnesota) |
| 1973 | Rod Carew (Minnesota) |
| 1974 | Rod Carew (Minnesota) |
| 1975 | Rod Carew (Minnesota) |
| 1976 | George Brett (Kansas City) |
| 1977 | Rod Carew (Minnesota) |
| 1978 | Rod Carew (Minnesota) |
| 1979 | Fred Lynn (Boston) |
| 1980 | George Brett (Kansas City) |

### NATIONAL LEAGUE

| Year | Name |
|---|---|
| 1949 | Jackie Robinson (Brooklyn) |
| 1950 | Stan Musial (St. Louis) |
| 1951 | Stan Musial (St. Louis) |
| 1952 | Stan Musial (St. Louis) |
| 1953 | Carl Furillo (Brooklyn) |
| 1954 | Willie Mayes (New York) |
| 1955 | Richie Ashburn (Philadelphia) |
| 1956 | Henry Aaron (Milwaukee) |
| 1957 | Stan Musial (St. Louis) |
| 1958 | Richie Ashburn (Philadelphia) |
| 1959 | Henry Aaron (Milwaukee) |
| 1960 | Dick Groat (Pittsburgh) |
| 1961 | Roberto Clemente (Pittsburgh) |
| 1962 | Tommy Davis (Los Angeles) |
| 1963 | Tommy Davis (Los Angeles) |
| 1964 | Roberto Clemente (Pittsburgh) |
| 1965 | Roberto Clemente (Pittsburgh) |
| 1966 | Matty Alou (Pittsburgh) |
| 1967 | Roberto Clemente (Pittsburgh) |
| 1968 | Pete Rose (Cincinnati) |
| 1969 | Pete Rose (Cincinnati) |
| 1970 | Rico Carty (Atlanta) |
| 1971 | Joe Torre (St. Louis) |
| 1972 | Billy Williams (Chicago) |
| 1973 | Pete Rose (Cincinnati) |
| 1974 | Ralph Garr (Atlanta) |
| 1975 | Bill Madlock (Chicago) |
| 1976 | Bill Madlock (Chicago) |
| 1977 | Dave Parker (Pittsburgh) |
| 1978 | Dave Parker (Pittsburgh) |
| 1979 | Keith Hernandez (St. Louis) |
| 1980 | Bill Buckner (Chicago) |

| Year | American League | Year | National League |
|------|-----------------|------|-----------------|
| 1981 | Carney Lansford (Boston) | 1981 | Bill Madlock (Chicago) |
| 1982 | Willie Wilson (Kansas City) | 1982 | Al Oliver (Montreal) |
| 1983 | Wade Boggs (Boston) | 1983 | Bill Madlock (Chicago) |
| 1984 | Don Mattingly (New York) | 1984 | Tony Gwynn (San Diego) |
| 1985 | Wade Boggs (Boston) | 1985 | Willie McGee (St. Louis) |
| 1986 | Wade Boggs (Boston) | 1986 | Tim Raines (Montreal) |
| 1987 | Wade Boggs (Boston) | 1987 | Tony Gwynn (San Diego) |
| 1988 | Wade Boggs (Boston) | 1988 | Tony Gwynn (San Diego) |
| 1989 | Kirby Puckett (Minnesota) | 1989 | Tony Gwynn (San Diego) |
| 1990 | George Brett (Kansas City) | 1990 | Willie McGee (St. Louis) |
| 1991 | Julio Franco (Texas) | 1991 | Terry Pendleton (Atlanta) |
| 1992 | Edgar Martinez (Seattle) | 1992 | Gary Sheffield (San Diego) |
| 1993 | John Olerud (Toronto) | 1993 | Andres Galarraga (Colorado) |
| 1994 | Paul O'Neill (New York) | 1994 | Tony Gwynn (San Diego) |
| 1995 | Edgar Martinez (Seattle) | 1995 | Tony Gwynn (San Diego) |
| 1996 | Alex Rodriguez (Seattle) | 1996 | Tony Gwynn (San Diego) |
| 1997 | Frank Thomas (Chicago) | 1997 | Tony Gwynn (Sand Diego) |
| 1998 | Bernie Williams (New York) | 1998 | Larry Walker (Colorado) |
| 1999 | Nomar Garciaparra (Boston) | 1999 | Larry Walker (Colorado) |

# SILVER SLUGGER AWARD

To form the Silver Slugger team, managers and coaches from each league choose nine players they would want in their lineup, based solely on performance at the plate. Their selections are based on a combination of offensive statistics for the season, such as batting average, slugging percentage and on-base percentage, and their general impressions of a player's overall offensive value. The coaches and managers are not allowed to vote for a player on their own team.

A representative of Hillerich & Bradsby presents the Silver Slugger award at a ceremony at the beginning of the following season. The trophy is three feet tall and bears the engraved names of all 18 winners from both leagues. Hillerich & Bradsby instituted the Silver Slugger award in 1980 as a natural extension of the Silver Bat award.

## SILVER SLUGGER TEAMS

| AMERICAN LEAGUE | | NATIONAL LEAGUE | |
|-----------------|--|-----------------|--|
| 1980 | Name | | Name |
| 1B | Cecil Cooper, Milwaukee | | Keith Hernandez, St. Louis |
| 2B | Willie Randolph, New York | | Manny Trillo, Philadelphia |
| 3B | George Brett, Kansas City | | Mike Schmidt, Philadelphia |
| SS | Robin Yount, Milwaukee | | Garry Templeton, St. Louis |
| OF | Ben Oglivie, Milwaukee | | Dusty Baker, Los Angeles |
| OF | Al Oliver, Texas | | Andre Dawson, Montreal |
| OF | Willie Wilson, Kansas City | | George Hendrick, St. Louis |
| C | Lance Parrish, Detroit | | Ted Simmons, St. Louis |
| DH | Reggie Jackson, New York | | |
| P | | | Bob Forsch, St. Louis |
| | | | |
| 1981 | | | |
| 1B | Cecil Cooper, Milwaukee | | Pete Rose, Philadelphia |
| 2B | Bobby Grich, California | | Manny Trillo, Philadelphia |
| 3B | Carney Lansford, Boston | | Mike Schmidt, Philadelphia |

*Crack of the Bat: The Louisville Slugger Story*

| 1981 (cont.) | American League | National League |
|---|---|---|
| SS | Rick Burleson, California | Dave Concepcion, Cincinnati |
| OF | Rickey Henderson, Oakland | Andre Dawson, Montreal |
| OF | Dave Winfield, New York | George Foster, Cincinnati |
| OF | | Dusty Baker, Los Angeles |
| C | Carlton Fisk, Chicago | Gary Carter, Montreal |
| DH | Al Oliver, Texas | |
| P | | Fernando Valenzuela, Los Angeles |

**1982**

| | American League | National League |
|---|---|---|
| 1B | Cecil Cooper, Milwaukee | Al Oliver, Montreal |
| 2B | Demaso Garcia, Toronto | Joe Morgan, San Francisco |
| 3B | Doug DeCinces, California | Mike Schmidt, Philadelphia |
| SS | Robin Yount, Milwaukee | Dave Concepcion, Cincinnati |
| OF | Dave Winfield, New York | Dale Murphy, Atlanta |
| OF | Willie Wilson, Kansas | Pedro Guerrero, Los Angeles |
| OF | Reggie Jackson, California | Leon Durham, Chicago |
| C | Lance Parrish, Detroit | Gary Carter, Montreal |
| DH | Hal McRae, Kansas City | |
| P | | Don Robinson, Pittsburgh |

**1983**

| | American League | National League |
|---|---|---|
| 1B | Eddie Murray, Baltimore | George Hendrick, St. Louis |
| 2B | Lou Whitaker, Detroit | Johnny Ray, Pittsburgh |
| 3B | Wade Boggs, Boston | Mike Schmidt, Philadelphia |
| SS | Cal Ripken, Jr., Baltimore | Dickie Thon, Houston |
| OF | Jim Rice, Boston | Andre Dawson, Montreal |
| OF | Dave Winfield, New York | Dale Murphy, Atlanta |
| OF | Lloyd Moseby, Toronto | Jose Cruz, Houston |
| C | Lance Parrish, Detroit | Terry Kennedy, San Diego |
| DH | Don Baylor, New York | |
| P | | Fernando Valenzuela, Los Angeles |

**1984**

| | American League | National League |
|---|---|---|
| 1B | Eddie Murray, Baltimore | Keith Hernandez, New York |
| 2B | Lou Whitaker, Detroit | Ryne Sandberg, Chicago |
| 3B | Buddy Bell, Texas | Mike Schmidt, Philadelphia |
| SS | Cal Ripken, Jr., Baltimore | Garry Templeton, San Diego |
| OF | Tony Armas, Boston | Dale Murphy, Atlanta |
| OF | Jim Rice, Boston | Jose Cruz, Houston |
| OF | Dave Winfield, New York | Tony Gwynn, San Diego |
| C | Lance Parrish, Detroit | Gary Carter, Montreal |
| DH | Andre Thornton, Cleveland | |
| P | | Rick Rhoden, Pittsburgh |

**1985**

| | American League | National League |
|---|---|---|
| 1B | Don Mattingly, New York | Jack Clark, St. Louis |
| 2B | Lou Whitaker, Detroit | Ryne Sandberg, Chicago |
| 3B | George Brett, Kansas | Tim Wallach, Montreal |
| SS | Cal Ripken, Jr., Baltimore | Hubie Brooks, Montreal |
| OF | Rickey Henderson, New York | Willie McGee, St. Louis |
| OF | Dave Winfield, New York | Dale Murphy, Atlanta |
| OF | George Bell, Toronto | Dave Parker, Cincinnati |
| C | Carlton Fisk, Chicago | Gary Carter, New York |
| DH | Don Baylor, New York | |
| P | | Rick Rhoden, Pittsburgh |

     *Crack of the Bat: The Louisville Slugger Story*

| 1986 | American League | National League |
|---|---|---|
| 1B | Don Mattingly, New York | Glenn Davis, Houston |
| 2B | Frank White, Kansas City | Steve Sax, Los Angeles |
| 3B | Wade Boggs, Boston | Mike Schmidt, Philadelphia |
| SS | Cal Ripken, Jr., Baltimore | Hubie Brooks, Montreal |
| OF | George Bell, Toronto | Tony Gwynn, Sand Diego |
| OF | Kirby Puckett, Minnesota | Tim Raines, Montreal |
| OF | Jesse Barfield, Toronto | Dave Parker, Cincinnati |
| C | Lance Parrish, Detroit | Gary Carter, New York |
| DH | Don Baylor, Boston | |
| P | | Rick Rhoden, Pittsburgh |

| 1987 | | |
|---|---|---|
| 1B | Don Mattingly, New York | Jack Clark, St. Louis |
| 2B | Lou Whitaker, Detroit | Juan Samuel, Philadelphia |
| 3B | Wade Boggs, Boston | Tim Wallach, Montreal |
| SS | Alan Trammell, Detroit | Ozzie Smith, St. Louis |
| OF | George Bell, Toronto | Andre Dawson, Chicago |
| OF | Dwight Evans, Boston | Eric Davis, Cincinnati |
| OF | Kirby Puckett, Minnesota | Tony Gwynn, Sand Diego |
| C | Matt Nokes, Detroit | Benito Santiago, San Diego |
| DH | Paul Molitor, Milwaukee | |
| P | | Bob Forsch, St. Louis |

| 1988 | | |
|---|---|---|
| 1B | George Brett, Kansas City | Andres Galarraga, Montreal |
| 2B | Julio Franco, Cleveland | Ryne Sandberg, Chicago |
| 3B | Wade Boggs, Boston | Bobby Bonilla, Pittsburgh |
| SS | Alan Trammell, Detroit | Barry Larkin, Cincinnati |
| OF | Kirby Puckett, Minnesota | Darryl Strawberry, New York |
| OF | Jose Canseco, Oakland | Andy Van Slyke, Pittsburgh |
| OF | Mike Greenwell, Boston | Kirk Gibson, Los Angeles |
| C | Carlton Fisk, Chicago | Benito Santiago, San Diego |
| DH | Paul Molitor, Milwaukee | |
| P | | Tim Leary, Los Angeles |

| 1989 | | |
|---|---|---|
| 1B | Fred McGriff, Toronto | Will Clark, San Francisco |
| 2B | Julio Franco, Texas | Ryne Sandberg, Chicago |
| 3B | Wade Boggs, Boston | Howard Johnson, New York |
| SS | Cal Ripken, Jr., Baltimore | Barry Larkin, Cincinnati |
| OF | Kirby Puckett, Minnesota | Kevin Mitchell, Sans Francisco |
| OF | Ruben Sierra, Texas | Tony Gwynn, San Diego |
| OF | Robin Yount, Milwaukee | Eric Davis, Cincinnati |
| C | Mickey Tettelton, Baltimore | Craig Biggio, Houston |
| DH | Harold Baines, Ch-Tex. | |
| P | | Don Robinson, San Francisco |

| 1990 | | |
|---|---|---|
| 1B | Cecil Fielder, Detroit | Eddie Murray, Los Angeles |
| 2B | Julio Franco, Texas | Ryne Sandberg, Chicago |
| 3B | Kelly Gruber, Toronto | Matt Williams, San Francisco |
| SS | Alan Trammell, Detroit | Barry Larkin, Cincinnati |
| OF | Rickey Henderson, Oakland | Barry Bonds, Pittsburgh |
| OF | Jose Canseco, Oakland | Bobby Bonilla, Pittsburgh |
| OF | Ellis Burks, Boston | Darryl Strawberry, New York |
| C | Lance Parrish, California | Benito Santiago, San Diego |
| DH | Dave Parker, Milwaukee | |
| P | | Don Robinson, San Francisco |

| 1991 | American League | National League |
|------|-----------------|-----------------|
| 1B | Cecil Fielder, Detroit | Will Clark, San Francisco |
| 2B | Julio Franco, Texas | Ryne Sandberg, Chicago |
| 3B | Wade Boggs, Boston | Howard Johnson, New York |
| SS | Cal Ripken, Jr., Baltimore | Barry Larkin, Cincinnati |
| OF | Jose Canseco, Oakland | Barry Bonds, Pittsburgh |
| OF | Joe Carter, Toronto | Bobby Bonilla, Pittsburgh |
| OF | Ken Griffey, Jr., Seattle | Ron Gant, Atlanta |
| C | Mickey Tettleton, Detroit | Benito Santiago, San Diego |
| DH | Frank Thomas, Chicago | |
| P | | Tom Glavine, Atlanta |

| 1992 | | |
|------|-----------------|-----------------|
| 1B | Mark McGwire, Oakland | Fred McGriff, San Diego |
| 2B | Roberto Alomar, Toronto | Ryne Sandberg, Chicago |
| 3B | Edgar Martinez, Seattle | Gary Sheffield, San Diego |
| SS | Travis Fryman, Detroit | Barry Larkin, Cincinnati |
| OF | Joe Carter, Toronto | Barry Bonds, Pittsburgh |
| OF | Juan Gonzalez, Texas | Andy Van Slyke, Pittsburgh |
| OF | Kirby Puckett, Minnesota | Larry Walker, Montreal |
| C | Mickey Tettleton, Detroit | Darren Daulton, Philadelphia |
| DH | Dave Winfield, Toronto | |
| P | | Dwight Gooden, New York |

| 1993 | | |
|------|-----------------|-----------------|
| 1B | Frank Thomas, Chicago | Fred McGriff, San Diego/Atlanta |
| 2B | Carlos Baerga, Cleveland | Robby Thompson, San Francisco |
| 3B | Wade Boggs, New York | Matt Williams, San Francisco |
| SS | Cal Ripken, Jr., Baltimore | Jay Bell, Pittsburgh |
| OF | Albert Belle, Cleveland | Barry Bonds, San Francisco |
| OF | Juan Gonzalez, Texas | Lenny Dykstra, Philadelphia |
| OF | Ken Griffey, Jr., Seattle | David Justice, Atlanta |
| C | Mike Stanley, New York | Mike Piazza, Los Angeles |
| DH | | |
| P | Dwight Gooden, New York | Orel Hershiser, Los Angeles |

| 1994 | | |
|------|-----------------|-----------------|
| 1B | Frank Thomas, Chicago | Jeff Bagwell, Houston |
| 2B | Carlos Baerga, Cleveland | Craig Biggio, Houston |
| 3B | Wade Boggs, New York | Matt Williams, San Francisco |
| SS | Cal Ripken, Jr., Baltimore | Wil Cordero, Montreal |
| OF | Albert Belle, Cleveland | Moises Alou, Montreal |
| OF | Ken Griffey, Jr., Seattle | Barry Bonds, San Francisco |
| OF | Kirby Puckett, Minnesota | Tony Gwynn, San Diego |
| C | Ivan Rodriguez, Texas | Mike Piazza, Los Angeles |
| DH | Julio Franco, Chicago | |
| P | | Mark Portugal, San Francisco |

| 1995 | | |
|------|-----------------|-----------------|
| 1B | Mo Vaughn, Boston | Eric Karros, Los Angeles |
| 2B | Chuck Knoblauch, Minnesota | Craig Biggio, Houston |
| 3B | Gary Gaetti, Kansas City | Vinny Castilla, Colorado |
| SS | John Valentin, Boston | Barry Larkin, Cincinnati |
| OF | Albert Belle, Cleveland | Dante Bichette, Colorado |
| OF | Tim Salmon, California | Tony Gwynn, San Diego |
| OF | Manny Ramirez, Cleveland | Sammy Sosa, Chicago |
| C | Ivan Rodriguez, Texas | Mike Piazza, Los Angeles |
| DH | Edgar Martinez, Seattle | |
| P | | Tom Glavine, Atlanta |

*Crack of the Bat: The Louisville Slugger Story*

| 1996 | *American League* | *National League* |
|------|-------------------|-------------------|
| 1B | Mark McGwire, Oakland | Andres Galarraga, Colorado |
| 2B | Roberto Alomar, Baltimore | Eric Young, Colorado |
| 3B | Jim Thome, Cleveland | Ken Caminiti, San Diego |
| SS | Alex Rodriguez, Seattle | Barry Larkin, Cincinnati |
| OF | Albert Belle, Cleveland | Ellis Burks, Colorado |
| OF | Ken Griffey, Jr., Seattle | Barry Bonds, Sand Francisco |
| OF | Juan Gonzalez, Texas | Gary Sheffield, Florida |
| C | Ivan Rodriguez, Texas | Mike Piazza, Los Angeles |
| DH | Paul Molitor, Minnesota | |
| P | | Tom Glavine, Atlanta |

| 1997 | | |
|------|---|---|
| 1B | Tino Martinez, New York Yankees | Jeff Bagwell, Houston Astros |
| 2B | Chuck Knoblauch, Minnesota Twins | Craig Biggio, Houston Astros |
| 3B | Matt Williams, Cleveland Indians | Vinny Castilla, Colorado Rockies |
| SS | Nomar Garciaparra, Boston Rex Sox | Jeff Blauser, Atlanta Braves |
| OF | Dave Justice, Cleveland Indians | Larry Walker, Colorado Rockies |
| OF | Ken Griffey, Jr., Seattle Mariners | Barry Bonds, San Francisco Giants |
| OF | Juan Gonzalez, Texas Rangers | Tony Gwynn, San Diego Padres |
| C | Ivan Rodriguez, Texas Rangers | Mike Piazza, Los Angeles Dodgers |
| DH | Edgar Martinez, Seattle Mariners | |
| P | | John Smoltz, Atlanta Braves |

| 1998 | | |
|------|---|---|
| 1B | Rafael Palmeiro, Baltimore Orioles | Mark McGwire, St. Louis Cardinals |
| 2B | Damion Easley, Detroit Tigers | Craig Biggio, Houston Astros |
| 3B | Dean Palmer, Kansas City Royals | Vinny Castilla, Colorado Rockies |
| SS | Alex Rodriguez, Seattle Mariners | Barry Larkin, Cincinnati Reds |
| OF | Ken Griffey, Jr., Seattle Mariners | Sammy Sosa, Chicago Cubs |
| OF | Albert Belle, Chicago White Sox | Moises Alou, Houston Astros |
| OF | Juan Gonzalez, Texas Rangers | Greg Vaughn, San Diego Padres |
| C | Ivan Rodriguez, Texas Rangers | Mike Piazza, New York Mets |
| DH | Jose Canseco, Toronto Blue Jays | |
| P | | Tom Glavine, Atlanta Braves |

| 1999 | | |
|------|---|---|
| 1B | Carlos Delgado, Toronto Blue Jays | Jeff Bagwell, Houston Astros |
| 2B | Roberto Alomar, Cleveland Indians | Edgardo Alfonzo, New York Mets |
| 3B | Dean Palmer, Detroit Tigers | Chipper Jones, Atlanta Braves |
| SS | Alex Rodriguez, Seattle Mariners | Barry Larkin, Cincinnati Reds |
| OF | Ken Griffey, Jr., Seattle Mariners | Sammy Sosa, Chicago Cubs |
| OF | Manny Ramirez, Cleveland Indians | Larry Walker, Colorado Rockies |
| OF | Shawn Green, Toronto Blue Jays | Vladimir Guerrero, Montreal Expos |
| C | Ivan Rodriguez, Texas Rangers | Mike Piazza, New York Mets |
| DH | Rafael Palmeiro, Texas Rangers | |
| P | | Mike Hampton, Houston Astros |

# BIBLIOGRAPHY

Adair, Robert K. *The Physics of Baseball.* 2nd ed. New York: HarperCollins, 1994.

Barney, Walter, ed. *A Celebration of Louisville Baseball in the Major and Minor Leagues.* Society for American Baseball Research. Pittsburgh, Pa.: Matthews Printing, 1997.

Erisfield, D. W. *Louisville Slugger Book of Great Hitters.* New York: John Wiley and Sons; New York: Mountain Lion, 1998.

Gutman, Dan. *Banana Bats & Ding-Dong Balls.* New York: Macmillan, 1995.

Malta, Vince, Ronald Fox, Bill Riddell, and Michael Specht. *Bats.* California: Fence Publishing, 1995.

Miller, Kori K., Lawrence W. Fielding, and Brenda G. Pitts. *The Rise of the Louisville Slugger in the Market Place.* Sports Marketing Quarterly, vol. 2, issue 3. Kentucky: University of Louisville, 1993.

Monteleone, John, and Mark Galo. *The Louisville Slugger Ultimate Book of Hitting.* New York: Henry Holt; New York: Mountain Lion, 1997.

Shatzkin, Mike, and Jim Charlton. *The Ballplayers.* New York: Arbor House; New York: William Morris, 1990.

*The Baseball Encyclopedia,* 10th ed. New York: Macmillan, 1996.

Voight, David Quentin. *The League That Failed.* Lanham, Md.: The Scarecrow Press, 1998.

Ward, Geoffrey C., and Ken Burns. *Baseball—An Illustrated History.* New York: Alfred A. Knopf, 1994.

*University of Louisville*
*Photographic Archives*

The Hillerich & Bradsby Photographic Collection at the University of Louisville Photographic Archives consists of nearly 4,000 black-and-white prints that fall into two broad categories. The first category consists of prints acquired by the Hillerich & Bradsby Co. as part of endorsement activities involving major and minor league baseball players, including team and individual portraits, award ceremonies, action photos, and winners of Hillerich & Bradsby Co.'s annual Silver Bat awards. The second category includes photographs commissioned by Hillerich & Bradsby that serve as documentation of the work of the company. These photographs show the steps involved in the production of baseball bats and golf clubs and also document visits to the Hillerich & Bradsby factory by many baseball teams and individual players. These photographs, which date from the 1920s through the 1950s, were donated to the University of Louisville by the Hillerich & Bradsby Co. beginning in 1986.

*University of Louisville*
*University Archives & Record Center*

The Hillerich & Bradsby Co. Collection at the University of Louisville Archives & Record Center consists of a body of advertising records donated by longtime employee and vice president of Advertising, Promotions and Public Relations for Hillerich & Bradsby, Jack McGrath. McGrath had collected the papers over the years with the hope of writing a history from them. The records include correspondence, legal papers, artwork, promotions, artifacts, publicity for both print and broadcast media to advertise the company's sports equipment, and clippings from newspapers, magazines, and trade publications. The items date from 1895 to 1979.

# IMAGE CREDITS

**FORWARD**
**PAGE** vii
National Baseball Hall of Fame Library &
Archive, Cooperstown, NY

**CHAPTER ONE**
**PAGE 2, 3**
University of Louisville Photographic
Archives–
R.G. Potter Collection

**PAGE 4**
University of Louisville University Archives &
Record Center, H&B Co. Collection

**PAGE 5**
National Baseball Hall of Fame Library &
Archive, Cooperstown, NY

**PAGE 6**
Louisville Slugger Museum–Pam Spaulding

**PAGE 7**
University of Louisville Photographic
Archives–
Caufield & Shook Collection
No. 188688

**PAGE 8 (LEFT)**
University of Louisville University Archives &
Record Center, H&B Co. Collection

**PAGE 8 (MIDDLE)**
University of Louisville University Archives &
Record Center, H&B Co. Collection

**PAGE 8 (RIGHT)**
University of Louisville University Archives &
Record Center, H&B Co. Collection

**PAGE 8 (BOTTOM)**
University of Louisville Photographic
Archives–
R.G. Potter Collection
No. 1022

**PAGE 9**
University of Louisville Photographic
Archives–
H&B Collection–
Geo Burke
No. 860

**PAGE 10**
"University of Louisville Photographic
Archives–R.G. Potter Collection
No. 1021

**PAGE 11 (LEFT)**
Courtesy of Mike McGrath

**PAGE 11 (RIGHT)**
H&B line of Louisville Slugger bats

University of Louisville Photographic
Archives–H&B Collection

**PAGE 12 (TOP)**
University of Louisville Photographic
Archives–
Sutcliffe Collection
No. 2088

**PAGE 12 (BOTTOM)**
University of Louisville Photographic
Archives–H&B Collection–
D.E. Polfrey
No. 1547

**PAGE 13**
Pam Spaulding

**PAGE 14**
Hillerich & Bradsby Co.

**PAGE 19**
Lou Sauritch

**CHAPTER TWO**
**PAGE 20, 21**
University of Louisville Photographic
Archives–H&B Collection–
Geo Burke
No. 1098

**PAGE 22**
Courtesy of Jay Kovar

**PAGE 23**
National Baseball Hall of Fame Library &
Archive, Cooperstown, NY

**PAGE 25**
National Baseball Hall of Fame Library &
Archive, Cooperstown, NY

**PAGE 27**
National Baseball Hall of Fame Library &
Archive, Cooperstown, NY

**PAGE 29**
National Baseball Hall of Fame Library &
Archive, Cooperstown, NY

**CHAPTER THREE**
**PAGE 30, 31**
University of Louisville Photographic
Archives–H&B Collection-
The Owens Studio
No. 3027

**PAGE 32**
Louisville Slugger Museum

**PAGE 33**
University of Louisville Photographic
Archives–R.G. Potter Collection

No. 2774

**PAGE 35**
Louisville Slugger Museum

**PAGE 36**
University of Louisville Photographic
Archives–R.G. Potter Collection
No. 6050

**PAGE 37**
University of Louisville Photographic
Archives–R.G. Potter Collection
No. 1042

**PAGE 39**
National Baseball Hall of Fame Library &
Archive, Cooperstown, NY

**PAGE 40 (TOP)**
University of Louisville Photographic
Archives–R.G. Potter Collection

**PAGE 40 (BOTTOM)**
Louisville Slugger Museum

**PAGE 41 (LEFT)**
University of Louisville University Archives &
Record Center, H&B Co. Collection

**PAGE 41 (RIGHT)**
University of Louisville Photographic
Archives–H&B Collection

**PAGE 42**
University of Louisville Photographic
Archives–H&B Collection–Tinsley Engraving
Co.
No. 484

**PAGE 43**
University of Louisville Photographic
Archives–H&B Collection
No. 559

**PAGE 44**
Pam Spaulding

**PAGE 45**
University of Louisville Photographic
Archives–H&B Collection–
Geo Burke
No. 3057

**PAGE 46**
Pam Spaulding

**PAGE 47**
Courier Journal/Louisville Times

**PAGE 49**
National Baseball Hall of Fame Library &
Archive, Cooperstown, NY